LIVING MISSION

BOOKS BY J. H. KROEGER

THE PHILIPPINE CHURCH AND EVANGELIZATION: 1965-1984.
Rome, Italy: Gregorian University Press, 1985.

ADVANCED CEBUANO COLLOQUIAL EXPRESSIONS.
Davao City, Philippines: Institute of Language and Culture, 1986.

CHURCH TRULY ALIVE: JOURNEY TO THE FILIPINO REVOLUTION.
Davao City, Philippines: Mission Studies Institute, 1988.

KNOWING CHRIST JESUS: A CHRISTOLOGICAL SOURCEBOOK.
Quezon City, Philippines: Claretian Publications, 1989.

INTERRELIGIOUS DIALOGUE: CATHOLIC PERSPECTIVES.
Davao City, Philippines: Mission Studies Institute, 1990.

MISSION TODAY: CONTEMPORARY THEMES IN MISSIOLOGY.
Hong Kong: Federation of Asian Bishops' Conferences, 1991.

LIVING MISSION

Challenges in Evangelization Today

James H. Kroeger, MM

with foreword by
Eugene LaVerdiere, SSS

ORBIS BOOKS
Maryknoll, New York 10545

CLARETIAN PUBLICATIONS
Quezon City, Philippines

LIVING MISSION
Challenges in Evangelization Today

Copyright © 1994 by James H. Kroeger

Published 1994 by
   Claretian Publications
   U.P. P.O. Box 4 Diliman, Quezon City, 1101
   Philippines
   Orbis Books
   Maryknoll, New York 10545

Claretian Publications is a pastoral endeavor of the Claretian Missionaries in the Philippines. It aims to promote a renewed spirituality rooted
in the process of total liberation and solidarity in response to the needs,
challenges and demands of the Church today.

The Catholic Foreign Mission Society of America (Maryknoll) recruits
and trains people for overseas missionary service. Through Orbis
Books, Maryknoll aims to foster the international dialogue that is
essential to mission. The books published, however, reflect the
opinions of their authors and are not meant to represent the official
position of the society.

Professional Services: Nancy Kennedy
Cover design: Alicia Grant

Library of Congress Cataloging-in-Publication Data

Kroeger, James H.
    Living Mission: Challenges in evangelization today / James H.
Kroeger : with foreword by Eugene LaVerdiere.
        p.   cm.
    Includes bibliographical references and index.
    ISBN 0–88344–921–8 (Orbis) : $16.95   971–501–588–3 (Claretian)
    1.   Catholic Church — Missions.   2.   Missions — Theory.
    3.   Evangelistic work — Philosophy.   4.   Christianity and other
religions.   I.   Title.
    BX2180.K6 1994
    266′.2—dc20   94-2788
                                                                      CIP

Contents

Preface

"Mission is an issue of faith." This sentence, hidden in the lengthy encyclical *Redemptoris Missio*, captures a pivotal insight into the reality of mission. Mission is directly related to the depth and vitality of one's faith convictions. A sense of the urgency of mission only springs from living faith.

The early Christians were fired with enthusiasm at Pentecost; they set out to the ends of the earth to give witness to their faith in Jesus as the crucified-risen Lord. Their faith and love of Jesus overcame great obstacles in preaching the Good News; they experienced a deepening in personal faith, precisely as they shared their faith with others. Without doubt, faith is always enriched when it is freely shared through love and witness.

Missionaries and evangelizers on all continents have welcomed the renewed emphasis in recent years on the centrality of mission in the life of the Church. This rededication to being a "community-in-mission" is a uniquely felt need in today's Church. Enthusiasm for mission based on deep faith convictions, however, appears to be in crisis in parts of the Church.

There is a well-known Chinese proverb: Crisis is a time of danger as well as a time of opportunity. One can view the current situation of mission in the Church as a time of impending doom or disaster. It is also possible to seize this moment as a missionary opportunity, joining Pope John Paul II who asserts that God is preparing a "new springtime for the

Gospel" and who foresees "the dawning of a new missionary age" (RM 86, 92).

This present work endeavors to contribute to the renewal of faith and enthusiasm for mission. Several approaches can facilitate this reawakening. Thus, this work examines mission, exploring its theological foundations, drawing insights from direct mission experience and offering reflections on mission spirituality. Summaries of key texts from the missionary writings of Popes Paul VI and John Paul II are presented.

No book emerges from a vacuum. And so with this one, a variety of experiences have shaped my perspectives on mission. I have served as a Maryknoll field missioner for over twenty years in the Philippines and Bangladesh. I have been privileged to engage in doctoral studies in missiology as well, and that has led me to reflect on what constitutes a properly theological and missiological foundation for the Church's missionary activity. These perspectives have been deepened from my study of recent mission documents of a variety of local Churches as they have reflected on the "universal" mission of the Church as a whole.

Several chapters have previously appeared in journals of missiology and spirituality. Minor repetition of central ideas will inevitably be found. Nevertheless, all chapters have been reworked and are refocused from the perspective of promoting a faith and spirituality which is foundational to any rekindling of missionary enthusiasm in the Church.

The words of Jesus in Luke's Gospel (4:43) express both his own consciousness as well as an urgent need in today's Church: "I must proclaim the Good News of the Kingdom of God to the other towns too, because that is what I was sent to do."

James H. Kroeger, M.M.
Mission Sunday – 1993

Foreword

"When I approach God in prayer, I do it in a Christian-Muslim manner." This is how Father James Kroeger describes his "hybrid" spirituality, developed over 20 years of experience in a Muslim culture, first on the island of Mindanao in the Philippines, then in Bangladesh. It is easy to identify with Father Kroeger's missionary experience of Islam.

The description evokes the personal memory of sunset in Izmir and the call to prayer, rising from dozens of minarets, echoing from mountainside to mountainside, slowly filling Izmir's great natural amphitheater. Looking on the ruins of Greco-Roman Smyrna, I thought of St. Polycarp and St. Ignatius of Antioch visiting on his way to martyrdom.

The description evokes another personal memory as well, of a visit long ago to one of Istanbul's great mosques. In the early afternoon, the mosque was very quiet, deserted except for a young man praying and chanting, kneeling with the book of the Qur'an open in front of him. Not wanting to interrupt something so beautiful, I watched and listened from a distance. I could not understand the words of his prayer, but remember very well the image of the young man absorbed in prayer. I also remember envying him.

Part missionary memoir, part theology, but all spirituality, the book reads like Father Kroeger's personal philosophy of life, with roots in the Scriptures, Vatican II and the recent teaching of the Holy See, of which he provides wonderful synopses.

We hear it on all sides today: "The Church is missionary by its very nature." But we do not see it on all sides. It may be that we are so overwhelmed with problems at home that we have no time for mission, forgetting that the solution to many of our problems lies precisely in having a strong sense of mission. For that, however, mission must not remain a matter of ideas, however clear and distinct, or of mere words, however wise and eloquent, but of life and reality.

Mission is a matter of the Word-made-flesh, human and mortal just like us, and of inculturation, that all may be one in Christ as he and the Father are one. Mission is a matter of Spirit, at work within us, announcing the Gospel of salvation and calling all peoples to *metanoia*. Mission is a matter of faith, love, hope and prayer, of sharing our deepest Christian and human values.

Mission is a matter of spirituality. In offering us his personal, deeply Christian and truly Catholic spirituality, Father Kroeger, a Maryknoll missionary among Muslim peoples, becomes a missionary to us, showing us what the Word-made-flesh, the Spirit of Christ, and the Gospel of salvation have meant for him and can mean for us.

Some things cannot be defined. One of those is God, whose name is revealed in the person of Jesus Christ. Another is the Church, with its mystery of communion in Christ and its mission to the ends of the earth. Actually, all those things that are most important in life, like life itself, being born from above and divine presence, cannot be defined. They can only be described as our experience of them deepens. Such things are the stuff of prayer and contemplation. Like enthusiasm, they cannot be taught, but they can be caught.

In a book, short in words and long in inspiration, Father Jim Kroeger reaches out to us as friends and invites us to catch his spirituality. Through this great, little book, may he become the friend of many.

Eugene LaVerdiere, SSS
Senior Editor, Emmanuel *Magazine*
Consultant for Education of Priests
*   and Seminarians, Society for the*
*   Propagation of the Faith*

Abbreviations

AA	–	*Apostolicam Actuositatem* (Apostolate of the Laity: November 18, 1965)
AAS	–	*Acta Apostolicae Sedis*
ADP	–	"Assisi Day of Prayer" (John Paul II: *Origins*: January 15, 1987, pp. 561-563)
AG	–	*Ad Gentes* (Missionary Activity: December 7, 1965)
CA	–	*Centesimus Annus* (On the Hundredth Anniversary of *Rerum Novarum*: May 1, 1991)
CELAM	–	*Consejo Episcopal Latinoamericano*
DM	–	*Dives in Misericordia* (On the Mercy of God: November 30, 1980)
D&M	–	*Dialogue and Mission* (Pontifical Council for Interreligious Dialogue: June 10, 1984)
D&P	–	*Dialogue and Proclamation* (Pontifical Council for Interreligious Dialogue: May 19, 1991)
DV	–	*Dominum et Vivificantem* (On the Holy Spirit in the Life of the Church and the World: May 18, 1986)
EE	–	*To the Ends of the Earth* (Pastoral Statement on World Mission—U.S.A. Bishops: November 13, 1986)
EMW	–	*Evangelization of the Modern World* (1974 Synod of Bishops Declaration: October 25, 1974)

EN   –   *Evangelii Nuntiandi* (Evangelization in the Modern World: December 8, 1975)

FABC   –   Federation of Asian Bishops' Conferences. Comprehensive collection of 1970-1991 Documents is: *For All the Peoples of Asia* (Orbis/Claretian), 1992.

FABC-OE   –   FABC: Office of Evangelization

GS   –   *Gaudium et Spes* (The Church in the Modern World: December 7, 1965)

LG   –   *Lumen Gentium* (The Church: November 21, 1964)

NA   –   *Nostra Aetate* (World Religions: October 28, 1965)

RH   –   *Redemptor Hominis* (Mystery of Redemption and Human Dignity: March 4, 1979)

RM   –   *Redemptoris Missio* (On the Permanent Validity of the Church's Missionary Mandate: December 7, 1990)

SD   –   *Salvifici Dolores* (On the Christian Meaning of Human Suffering: February 11, 1984)

UR   –   *Unitatis Redintegratio* (Ecumenism: November 21, 1964)

Overviews of Mission

Springtime in Mission

Mission statistics of the 1990s confront Christian churches in a dramatic and disturbing way. Consider: Christians of all denominations are only one-third of the world's population. Before the year 2000, Islam will claim more followers than Roman Catholicism, currently the world's single largest religion; Asia, where 60 percent of the human race lives, is less than two percent Christian. More than 23 percent of all peoples have never come into contact with Christianity, Christ or the Gospel.

Why should Catholics want to answer these challenges? While there is much discussion and many publications from the churches, at least 99 percent of these address only Christian interests. Of all foreign missionaries, 91 percent target populations in the Christian world with 90 percent of all evangelization efforts directed toward those who are at least nominally Christian. Only 3 percent of all Christians have contact with people of other faiths. An embarrassing fact is that the Christian world spends 99 percent of its income on itself.

These mission statistics, drawn from respected Catholic and Protestant sources, underscore the urgency behind Pope John Paul II's recent mission encyclical: *Redemptoris Missio* (The Mission of the Redeemer). The Pope asserts: "Missionary activity specifically directed *ad gentes* (to the nations) appears to be waning." This fact "must arouse concern among all who believe in Christ." Why? Because "... in the Church's history, missionary drive has always been a sign of vitality, just as its lessening is a sign of a crisis of faith" (2).

The Pope urges a "fresh impulse to missionary activity," the deepening of "commitment of the particular churches," and the harnessing of "all of the Church's energies to a new evangelization" (2-3). In a word, the focus of John Paul is direct and clear: "I wish to invite the church to *renew her missionary commitment*" (2).

Capturing the highlights of a lengthy document – and doing it in inviting language – is a formidable task, but the effort must be made since the Pope summons, *"Peoples everywhere, open the doors to Christ!"* (3).

VISION OF EVANGELIZATION

What view of evangelization emerges from a comprehensive analysis of the encyclical? Repeatedly, the document speaks of mission, evangelization and salvation in a holistic fashion: "Jesus came to bring integral salvation, one which embraces the whole person... " (11); "evangelical witness... is directed towards integral human development" (42); "action on behalf of integral development and liberation... is most urgently needed" (58).

Integral evangelization, as repeatedly affirmed in the encyclical (20, 41-60), reflects current missiological thought as well as recent magisterial teaching. Paul VI in *Evangelii Nuntiandi* clearly encouraged Catholics to view mission holistically. The second chapter of *Evangelii Nuntiandi* speaks of the complexity of the evangelizing action and its various complementary and mutually enriching elements.

Another Roman document, issued by the Secretariat for Non-Christians (now called the Pontifical Council for Interreligious Dialogue), which elucidates the holistic approach to evangelization and salvation appeared on Pentecost Sunday, 1984. Entitled: "The Attitude of the Church toward the Followers of Other Religions: Reflections and Orientations on Dialogue and Mission," this source affirms that mission is presented "in the consciousness of the Church as a single but complex and articulated reality" (13); the new encyclical echoes this vision: "Mission is a single but complex reality, and it develops in a variety of ways" (41). Again, "mission is one and undivided, having one origin and one final purpose; but within it, there are different tasks and kinds of activity" (31).

The vision of mission that the Pope urges remains focused on integral evangelization; it is not a narrow, anti-pagan (much less anti-Muslim) crusade as one early press release charged.

The fifth chapter of *Redemptoris Missio*, labeled "The Paths of Mission," views mission *holistically*. Key dimensions are: the witness of Christian living, the service of humanity, inculturation and interreligious dialogue, explicit gospel proclamation, and sacramental-liturgical-ecclesial life. All these elements are part and parcel of the Church's total mission of evangelization and follow the example of Jesus who lived mission in silence, in action, in dialogue, in teaching, and in prayer.

FOUNDATIONAL MISSION THEOLOGY

This mission encyclical, which commemorates the twenty-fifth anniversary of *Ad Gentes*, clearly affirms the foundations of mission theology and the centrality and urgency of mission in the life of the Church.

The years following the Second Vatican Council were a golden opportunity to explore and debate, renew and clarify the Church's mission; and, it is true that "The Council has already borne much fruit in the realm of missionary activity.... Above all, there is a new awareness that *missionary activity is a matter for all Christians*" (2). Yet, at this time John Paul also discerned a need to reaffirm diverse aspects of the Catholic Church's foundational theology of Christian mission.

At least one third of the encyclical (three chapters out of eight) deals with theological questions. Chapter One includes core elements of the dogmatic theology of Revelation and Faith, Christology and Soteriology, as well as Ecclesiology and Missiology. Chapter Two focuses on biblical theology, particularly the kingdom of God. And, to the delight of missiologists, Chapter Three is completely devoted to pneumatology, examining the role of the Holy Spirit in the life of the Church and its mission.

The following are key emphases in the opening chapter: [1] All mission is centered in God's wonderful, generous loving plan of salvation *(mysterion)*, made known through Jesus and accepted in faith. Jesus is the "definitive self-revelation of God" and "the fundamental reason why the Church is missionary by her very nature" (5). [2] While affirming with the Scriptures (I Tim. 2:4) the universality of salvation, "the Church believes that God has established Christ as the one mediator and that it has been established as the universal sacrament of salvation" (9). [3] The Pope unhesitatingly reaffirms these basics of Church teaching, noting that *"Mission is an issue of faith"* (11).

The biblical theme of the kingdom *(basileia)* is the integrating leitmotif of the second chapter. Preaching the kingdom and promoting its values are the missionary tasks of the Church which is "effectively and concretely at the service of the Kingdom" (20). The encyclical offers clarity and interpretation on other dimensions of kingdom theology: the kingdom of God and the Christ-event are complementary proclamations (16); the kingdom necessarily has a transcendent horizon (17); the kingdom "cannot be detached either from Christ or from the Church" (18); theocentrism and ecclesiocentrism demand a nuanced critique which is consistent with Church teaching (17-18).

Currently, the theology of the Holy Spirit (pneumatology) is of particular interest to missiologists and missionaries alike. "The Holy Spirit is indeed the principal agent of the whole of the Church's mission. The Holy Spirit's action is preeminent in mission *ad gentes* (21). The Spirit's centrality is emphasized because the Holy Spirit's "presence and activity affect not only individuals but also society and history, peoples, cultures and religions" (28). Ask any missionary and you will receive an eloquent personal testimony of the presence and power of the Spirit active in peoples, cultures, and religions – renewing the face of the earth! The acts of today's apostles continuously write the gospel of the Holy Spirit!

TRANSMITTING THE URGENCY OF MISSION

The English title given to John Paul II's mission encyclical is: "On the Permanent Validity of the Church's Missionary Mandate." Thus, mission is always and everywhere essential; it is "not considered a marginal task for the Church but is situated at the center of her life, as a fundamental commitment of the whole People of God" (32). Mission is "the greatest and holiest duty of the Church" (63). The Pope's affirmations resonate throughout the work: "I have chosen to travel to the ends of the earth in order to show this missionary concern" (1); "mission *ad gentes* is still in its infancy" (40); "I see the dawning of a new missionary age" (92).

No one seeks to minimize the Pope's assertions about the centrality and urgency of mission; however, it is a valid question to ask about strategies for implementation. Words of exhortation must give way to programs of concrete actualization. In the considered judgment of this author, the encyclical is strong on the *why* of mission, but is only moderately successful on the *how*.

Mission animation – the *how* of mission – requires continued discussion. While it is best accomplished locally, one can highlight some creative suggestions found within the encyclical.

The Christian family is a key and irreplaceable force in mission motivation (42); this insight is consistent with the teaching of Vatican II which termed the family the "domestic church" (LG 11). Promoting Christian family life should redound to mission awareness and animation. Material and financial donations are gratefully received, yet families are challenged to offer "a special contribution to the missionary cause of the Church by fostering missionary vocations among their sons and daughters" (80).

John Paul challenges Christians: Do you wish to promote mission? True disciples are urged to "carry out a sincere review of their lives regarding their solidarity with the poor" (60). As followers of Jesus, "we should reassess our own way of living" (81); "Fight hunger by changing your lifestyle" (59); "We cannot preach conversion unless we ourselves are converted anew every day" (47).

The role of missionary institutes and societies is crucial in mission animation; missionaries themselves should continue their "radical and total self-giving," initiate "new and bold endeavors," and "not allow themselves to be daunted by doubts, misunderstanding, rejection or persecution" (66). Diocesan seminarians and priests "must have the mind and heart of missionaries" (67). The Church must seek to expand the spheres "in which lay people are present and active as missionaries" (72). Missionary dynamism should become contagious!

Youth involvement is essential to lasting mission animation. They should be offered opportunities to visit overseas missions, to meet and offer hospitality to non-Christians and migrants within their own country (82). The idealism of youth is a potential resource – their rejection of violence and war, their desire for freedom and justice, their rejection of racism and closed nationalism, their affirmation of the dignity and role of women (86). The vision of Charles de Foucauld (as a "universal brother") can fire the imagination of youth (89), can be a path toward missionary commitment.

ADDITIONAL MAJOR EMPHASES

An author seeking to compose a popular synthesis of a papal encyclical faces the challenge of providing a balanced presentation. This writer sees several other major emphases within the work. A paragraph is devoted to each.

Local churches around the world are the central actors in mission today; all evangelization necessarily is harmoniously accomplished in, with, and through the local church which is responsible for the totality of mission. This is a sea change in the dynamics of mission; both local churches and missionaries alike must explore the ramifications of this new reality. Many leads are found in the encyclical (26, 30, 39, 48-52, 62-64, 71, 83-85, 92).

Missionary activity is not an external imposition which violates human dignity and freedom. Or again, witnessing and proclaiming Christ are not at odds with people's dignity as persons or their freedom of conscience (7-8). Authentic mission does not restrict freedom, but rather seeks to advance it; the document is clear: *"The Church proposes; she imposes nothing"* (39).

Individuals who receive the permanent, life-long vocation to foreign, transcultural mission are a treasured resource of the Church. Their vocation is necessary for the Church (32); it is a unique calling (27, 65); it is the model of the Church's missionary commitment (66); it is to be assiduously cultivated (79, 84), particularly by mission institutes themselves (65-66).

The encyclical looks positively upon interreligious dialogue, devoting several sections to presenting it comprehensively (55-57). Interfaith dialogue "is part of the Church's evangelizing mission,... is not in opposition to the mission of *Ad Gentes,...* [and] *does not dispense from evangelization.*" This same section speaks of God's call to all peoples and his presence to them "of which their religions are the main and essential expression." The Church's reverence for the followers of other faiths and religions is clearly affirmed by the encyclical; it is not a "turning back the clock" as some critics may purport.

Women receive the Pope's praise and gratitude for their outstanding contribution to mission: "I extend a special word of appreciation to the missionary Religious sisters" (70); "How can we forget the important role played by women"? (71). "It is necessary to recognize – and it is a title of honor – that some Churches owe their origins to the activity of lay men and women missionaries" (71).

The process of inculturation and its relationship to mission receives extensive treatment (25, 52-54, 76). Authentic evangelization involves the Church in the inculturation process, an "intimate transformation of authentic cultural values through their integration in Christianity and the insertion of Christianity in the various human cultures." This task is never finished and today it encounters new challenges – especially in large cities, "where new customs and styles of living arise together with new forms of culture and communication" (37). Mission and inculturation demand fresh initiatives and creativity in the techtronic age of the megapolis!

The entire final chapter of *Redemptoris Missio* treats "missionary spirituality" (87-91). Four elements characterize Jesus' disciples-be-come-missionary; the missionary is to be led by the Spirit, to live the mystery of Christ who himself was sent, to love the Church and humanity as Jesus did, and to desire the holiness of saints. In a word, mission spirituality is "a journey towards holiness" and the success of renewing the urgency of the Church's missionary impulse "demands holy missionaries."·

PRECIOUS DETAILS – NOT TO BE LOST

In a work as long as this papal mission encyclical one would expect to find details that demand further reflection. Any synthesis presentation must take note of them.

The personalist philosophy and orientation of John Paul II is manifested throughout the work. The person is always central in diverse mission apostolates, in work for justice (42), in fostering interreligious dialogue (55-57), in promoting development; the human person "is the principal agent of development, not money or technology" (58). In uniquely personalist terms, the missionary is described as "a person of the Beatitudes" (91) and it is love that is always *"the driving force of mission"* (60).

The encyclical profusely expresses the Church's gratitude to its missionaries (2, 57, 60, 70). The Church's theologians provide an important service to the cause of mission (36) and should promote the study of world religions and science of missiology (83). The church needs a renewed commitment to ecumenism within mission (50).

In looking at today's world from the viewpoint of evangelization, the document distinguishes three situations: "non-Christian" peoples, Christians requiring pastoral care, and the so-called "post-Christians"; all require special approaches (32-34). Geographically, the Pope emphasizes the missionary demands within Asia (37, 55, 91).

The theology of the "implantation of the Church" (*plantatio Ecclesiae)* is specifically mentioned twice (49, 72). This approach is not inimical to mission when read with the full ecclesiology of the documents of Vatican II. Its pastoral implementation is served well by the basic ecclesial communities as a force for evangelization (51).

Significant and surprising is the fact that one unique quote appears verbatim no less than three times in the text (6, 10, 28): "we are obliged to hold that the Holy Spirit offers everyone the possibility of sharing in the Paschal Mystery in a manner known to God." Certainly, one cannot mistake the Pope's assertion that God's loving plan for salvation includes each and every person!

Mission as "God's work" (24) is clearly affirmed; it is based "not on human abilities but on the power of the Risen Lord" (23). Missionaries are conscious that they owe their faith and vocations "not to their own merits but to Christ's special grace" (11). They must believe that "it is not we who are the principal agents of the Church's mission, but Jesus Christ and his Spirit" (36). A missioner's faith journey "proceeds along *the path* already trodden by the Virgin Mary" (92).

Fifteen years ago Pope Paul VI wrote that "Modern man listens more willingly to witnesses than to teachers, and if he does listen to teachers, it is because they are witnesses" (EN 41). This passage is recalled in *Redemptoris Missio* (42). It must continue to remain a central focus if the Church wishes to respond "with generosity and holiness to the calls and challenges of our time" (92). In simplicity and profundity, the entire Church prays with constantly renewed vigor and urgency: *Veni Creator Spiritus.*

Mission Through Dialogue

Pentecost 1991 brought Catholic evangelizers a Spirit-filled gift – a new missionary document with the title: *Dialogue and Proclamation*. This gift follows the pope's mission encyclical by only a few months, making 1991 a "bumper-crop year" in mission awareness. Both documents are imperative resources for grasping the meaning of contemporary mission, especially in the Asian context.

Dialogue and Proclamation does not stand in isolation from the renewal in mission thought begun by Vatican II. This quarter-century exploration has followed an enlightening trajectory: Vatican II decrees on mission *(Ad Gentes)* and religions *(Nostra Aetate)*, Paul VI's exhortation on evangelization *(Evangelii Nuntiandi)*, the Secretariat for Non-Christians' 1984 masterpiece *(Dialogue and Mission)*, and John Paul II's encyclical *(Redemptoris Missio)*. These six resources form the core of the universal Church's recent magisterium on mission and evangelization.

Two Roman bodies cooperated to issue *Dialogue and Proclamation*; the Pontifical Council for Interreligious Dialogue initiated the work and received the collaboration of the Congregation for the Evangelization of Peoples. This joint effort produced a valuable vademecum for evangelizers, particularly those who serve peoples of other living faith traditions.

DIALOGUE INTEGRATES MISSION

John Paul II treated dialogue with our brothers and sisters of other religions in *Redemptoris Missio* (55-57). The pope noted that "Interreligious dialogue is a part of the Church's evangelizing mission... The Church sees no conflict between proclaiming Christ and engaging in interreligious dialogue." This latest document, standing in continuity with the encyclical (4), affirms and elaborates the necessity of dialogue and its relationship to proclamation.

Although some churchpersons "fail to see the value of interreligious dialogue," it is gaining ground and "gradually coming to be understood" (4). In today's world with rapid communication, mobility and interdependence, a new awareness of religious plurality has emerged; world religious traditions and their adherents demand a sensitive response from Christians. And, the best response is captured in the very title of the document under consideration – dialogue and proclamation. As John Paul II has noted, "There can be no question of choosing one and ignoring or rejecting the other" (6).

Dialogue is not a mere decoration or technique of pre-evangelization. It is "one of the integral elements of the Church's evangelizing mission" (9). Again, dialogue along with proclamation are to be viewed as "component elements and authentic forms of the one evangelizing mission of the Church" (2). In a word, interreligious dialogue has found its home within the church's evangelizing mission (33-41). Parenthetically, the nuances of the above assertions are enhanced by careful reading of the sections clarifying these terms: evangelization (8), dialogue (9), proclamation (10), conversion (11), religions and religious traditions (12-13).

It is important to note that underlying this positive evaluation of dialogue within the church's mission is a vision of evangelization that is best described as comprehensive, integral and holistic. In accepting that the church's evangelizing mission is a "single but complex and articulated reality," one consequently understands that the "principle elements" of mission are "presence and witness; commitment to social development and human liberation; liturgical life, prayer and contemplation; interreligious dialogue; and finally, proclamation and catechesis" (2). Stated succinctly, all mission envisions integral evangelization (2, 8, 55, 75, 76). Jesus himself accomplished his Abba-given mission in this holistic manner (21-23, 55).

If Jesus' mission and the church's continuance of it are viewed holistically, then dialogue-within-mission will refer to "all positive and constructive interreligious relations with individuals and communities of other faiths which are directed at mutual understanding and enrichment" (9). The church is firmly and irreversibly committed to promoting and enhancing this multi-faceted dialogue (54).

ATTITUDES ARE PIVOTAL

The Pentecost 1984 document from the Vatican Secretariat for Non-Christians (now known as the Pontifical Council for Interreligious Dialogue) bore the cumbersome yet descriptive title: "The Attitude of the Church toward the Followers of Other Religions: Reflections and Orientations on Dialogue and Mission." By focusing on the church's "attitude" toward those whom she approaches in mission, a pivotal theme in dialogue is identified. In short, all authentic dialogue demands an "attitude of respect" which must "permeate all those activities constituting the evangelizing mission of the Church" (9). The task of promoting a *renewed dialogical outlook* is a key purpose of both the 1984 and 1991 Pentecost documents. This task is Herculean and requires enough faith to conquer many diverse difficulties (52).

A closer look at the "attitudes" essential to dialogue will prove enlightening. One does well to begin with a realistic view of the challenge of dialogue: "Already on a purely human level it is not easy to practice dialogue. Interreligious dialogue is even more difficult" (51). History is replete with religious conflicts, cultural and ethnic domination, territorial wars and destruction – an endless list is possible. Yet, herein lies the church's commitment to the Kingdom and to transforming biased and prejudicial attitudes. Yes, challenges abound, but "the obstacles,

though real, should not lead us to underestimate the possibilities of dialogue or to overlook the results already achieved" (54).

Positively, dialogue requires "a balanced attitude" that is "open and receptive" and it demands "unselfishness and impartiality, acceptance of differences and of possible contradictions. The will to engage together in commitment to the truth and the readiness to allow oneself to be transformed by the encounter are other dispositions required" (47).

Dialogue does not mean the abandonment of one's religious convictions. On the contrary, one enters dialogue precisely as a religious person; "the sincerity of interreligious dialogue requires that each enters into it with the integrity of his or her own faith" (48).

Christians accept God's self-manifestation to the followers of other religious traditions; thus, Jesus' followers experience that "Far from weakening their own faith, true dialogue will deepen it.... Their faith will gain new dimensions as they discover the active presence of the mystery of Jesus Christ beyond the visible boundaries of the Church and of the Christian fold" (50).

Indeed, the success of dialogue within the Church's evangelizing mission requires nothing less than radical attitudinal conversion. This fact cannot be overemphasized (cf. 47-54, 83); in addition, it is "an unending process" (49). Dialogue demands commitment and transformation!

DIALOGUE VIS-A-VIS PROCLAMATION

The structure of this document is simple and clearly focused. After an introduction which contextualizes the debate (1-13), a lengthy treatment is given to "interreligious dialogue" (14-54) and to "proclaiming Jesus Christ" (55-76). Then, dialogue and proclamation are studied in their mutual relationships (77-86). A brief conclusion (87-89) rounds out the presentation.

A few descriptive passages capture the current understanding of the dynamics of the dialogue-proclamation relationship. Though not on the same level, both are "authentic elements of the Church's evangelizing mission. Both are legitimate and necessary. They are intimately related, but not interchangeable: true interreligious dialogue on the part of the Christian supposes the desire to make Jesus Christ better known, recognized and loved; proclaiming Jesus Christ is to be carried out in the Gospel spirit of dialogue" (77).

Continuing the clarification, the document notes that "All Christians are called to be personally involved in these two ways of carrying out the one mission of the Church, namely proclamation and dialogue.... They must nevertheless always bear in mind that dialogue, as has already been said, does not constitute the whole mission of the Church, that it cannot simply replace proclamation, but remains ori-

ented towards proclamation in so far as the dynamic process of the
Church's evangelizing mission reaches in it its climax and its fullness"
(82).

Holding dialogue and proclamation in a harmonious, fruitful
tension is a delicate balancing act. Yet, that is precisely what local
churches and missionaries are asked to achieve (43, 78, 82). There are
clear obstacles to be faced both in dialogue (51-54) as well as in
proclamation (72-74). Evangelizers through prayer and the Eucharist
will be able to "draw the grace of discernment, to be able to read the
signs of the Spirit's presence and to recognize the favorable time and
right manner of proclaiming Jesus Christ" (86).

ADDITIONAL GEMS

This medium-length document was five years in preparation; it contains
many insightful and reflective treasures. Several items are discussed
here by devoting one paragraph to each theme.

The reality of *conversion* is best understood as a dynamic process
on two levels. Mission always includes a call to open one's heart to an
experience of the living God (11, 41). This call is to all peoples –
Christians included (32). Based on this general or foundational conversion, one may also be called in conscience "to leave one's previous
spiritual or religious situation" (41), "to a change of religious adherence" (11). Today's evangelizers need great sensitivity in interpreting
the workings of God's grace in their own lives and in the lives of the
followers of other faiths.

Current mission thought rightly places important emphasis on the
theology of the Holy Spirit (pneumatology). John Paul II's mission
encyclical devoted an entire chapter to "The Holy Spirit, the Principle
Agent of Mission." *Dialogue and Proclamation* continues this
pneumatological thematic (17, 21, 26, 29, 35, 64-65, 68-69, 84, 86, 89).
In God's loving plan of salvation, the universal action of the Holy Spirit
is operative in the world, and interreligious dialogue becomes an
important key to discovering the Spirit's befriending presence. Today,
all Christian mission must possess "a universality which is both
Christological and Pneumatological in character" (21).

An important concept of Paul VI, a truly missionary pope, appears
in several places in this document. Affirming the centrality of dialogue

in the Church's mission, Paul VI always spoke of interreligious inter-action as a "dialogue of salvation" (38-39, 67, 80). When peoples of diverse faiths interact to search for the divine will, God is in dialogue with these believers; thus, "interreligious dialogue is truly part of the dialogue of salvation initiated by God" (80). Current efforts in dialogue affirm that "God, in an age-long dialogue, has offered and continues to offer salvation to humankind" (38; cf. 53).

One special quote from Vatican II has gained ascendancy in current papal teaching on mission and dialogue. For example, it appeared verbatim three times in *Redemptoris Missio* (6, 10, 28); John Paul II used it to explain the meaning of the 1986 World Day of Prayer for Peace in Assisi. It reappears here in *Dialogue and Proclamation* in three places (15, 28, 68). The quote – so pregnant with reflective meaning and insight – reads as follows: "we are obliged to hold that the Holy Spirit offers everyone the possibility of sharing in this Paschal Mystery in a manner known to God" (GS 22).

The Pontifical Council for Interreligious Dialogue has issued two major documents in recent years: Pentecost of 1984 and of 1991. A special theme common to both works focuses on "the patience of God" in the church's commitment to dialogue. "Much patience is required" (53) to engage in dialogue and proclamation! "All, both Christians and the followers of other religious traditions, are invited by God himself to enter into the mystery of his patience" (84; cf. Pentecost of 1984 document, No. 44). Any seasoned missioner, particularly in the Asian context, will attest to the validity of this insight.

A SECOND LOOK

In assessing *Dialogue and Proclamation*, a few evaluative comments are offered.

This document is written in the same creative style as *Dialogue and Mission* (Pentecost, 1984). Each numbered paragraph is preceded by a phrase which summarizes the central idea of that paragraph. When all these phrases are read continuously, they form a series of sentences summarizing the whole document. This approach results in a succinct overview of the main content of the entire work; it is both helpful and creative.

As a piece which has dialogue as one main theme, the document sensitively avoids giving offense by its choice of language. For example, the negative term "Non-Christian" is avoided; when all people are the subject of discussion, inclusive language is employed (e.g. 28, 48). This is a direction to be encouraged.

Writing as an Asian missioner, this author laments that the excellent work and reflective insights of the Asian local churches are not included in this work – even in the endnotes. Asian bishops, theologians and missioners have many treasures to share about interreligious dialogue; they are drawn from their lived experience, they are theologically rich, they are creatively and competently expressed. The "Theses on Interreligious Dialogue" prepared by the Theological Advisory Commission of the Federation of Asian Bishops' Conferences (FABC) are one example of the competent work done by the local churches in Asia. Such work deserves recognition.

Dialogue and Proclamation, with its subtitle, "Reflections and Orientations on Interreligious Dialogue and the Proclamation of the Gospel of Jesus Christ," stands as an integrated whole. Its content is enlightening and carefully written. If forced to recommend some sections, this writer would draw attention to the definition of terms (8-13), the place of dialogue in mission (33-41), and the manner of proclamation (68-71).

This lengthy overview has sought to whet readers' appetites to explore the riches of *Dialogue and Proclamation*. It now concludes with a reminder and an exhortation: "Dialogue and proclamation are difficult tasks, and yet absolutely necessary" (89); "All Christians are called to be personally involved in these two ways of carrying out the one mission of the Church, namely proclamation and dialogue" (82).

Theological Foundations

Aware We Are Sent

Adequately capturing realities in the spiritual life always demands the use of dynamic, expansive language. For this reason, spirituality is frequently described in relational categories – between a disciple and the master, between a Christian and a personal God, between the servant-herald and the crucified-risen Lord. Such a relationship of intimacy is at the heart of biblical spirituality: "I will be your God and you shall be my people" (Ex. 19:4-6; Lev. 26:12; Deut. 7:6-9; Jer. 11:4; Jer. 30:22); Christians are Jesus' friends (Jn. 15:15) and call their heavenly Father "Abba" (Rom. 8:15; Gal. 4:6).

Spirituality may also variously be described in terms of a growth-process, an evolution toward maturity, a pilgrimage. Each descriptive category attempts to present an authentic, albeit partial, grasp of the human-divine dynamic operative in our lives. In this piece, "conscious-ness" or "awareness" forms the framework to enhance our insight into spirituality. And, this category naturally overflows with an apostolic or missionary dynamism!

CONSCIOUSNESS: A WINDOW INTO SPIRITUALITY

Consciousness may seem to be an elusive concept; yet, no one would deny the reality. An individual is in a conscious state when perceptual and cognitive faculties are functioning normally. One continuously synthesizes various stimuli from within and from without; ideally, the result is a healthy personal integration.

Notice that a whole panorama of constitutive elements are included within the framework of consciousness. Diverse aspects of conscious awareness derive from one's seeing, hearing, feeling, thinking, desiring, experiencing. Consciousness incorporates perceptions, emotions, observations, thoughts, aspirations, choices. It also includes an introspective awareness of the personal impact of all events and experience.

In light of this brief and rudimentary description of the phenomenon of human consciousness, one may begin to elaborate the relationship between consciousness and a spirituality of the apostolate. Our faith-life derives much profit from prayer, reflection, experience, service – all focused on raising our God-consciousness and expanding the horizons of our spiritual awareness. We want to use our eyes to see perceptively and our ears to hear attentively (Mk. 8:18); we hope to gain deepened insight into our lives through faith's mirror (Jas. 1:22-25).

In another vein, a look at the venerable Eastern traditions of many Asian nations reveals that the man of God or the God-conscious/God-focused person is essentially a seer, sage, or mystic. Such a person "sees" and experiences God; God is not an object of knowledge, but a subject of experience. To grow in holistic spirituality is concomitant with an experiential awareness and consciousness of God's presence and activity in all dimensions of one's life.

The beautiful prayer in the *Upanishads*, one of the Hindu sacred books, expresses the aspiration and spiritual desire to come to this deeper conscious union with the divine. In Sanskrit and English it is:

> "Asato ma satgamaya
> Tamaso ma jyotir gamaya
> Mrutyu ma amrutam gamaya."

> "God, lead me from untruth to truth
> Lead me from darkness to light
> Lead me from death to immortality."

Thomas Merton, the Trappist monk and spiritual writer (1915-1968), has enabled countless people gain insights into their spirituality. Merton intimately links spirituality and prayer with the transformation of consciousness. He sees that a renewed conscious awareness under-lies all spiritual growth; each Christian must cease to assert one's self as the center of consciousness and discover God's presence as the deepest center of consciousness within him. Thus, as one's self-consciousness changes, the individual is transformed; one's self is no longer its own center; it is now centered on God.

It is important to note that for Merton no one will ever be capable of communion with God and others without this deep awakening, this transformation of consciousness. Such transformative growth, as ex-plained by Merton, "consists in a double movement: man's entering into the deepest center of himself, and then, after passing through that center, going out of himself to God" (Higgins, 49).

In addition, Merton asserts that unless our spirituality and prayer "does something to awaken in us a consciousness of our union with God, of our complete dependence upon Him for all our vital acts in the spiritual life, and of His constant loving presence in the depths of our souls, it has not achieved the full effect for which it is intended" (Merton-A, 67). Or again, Merton holds that in today's world: "What is required of Christians is that they develop a completely modern and contempo-rary *consciousness* in which their experience as men of our century is integrated with their experience as children of God redeemed by Christ" (Merton-B, 279).

The renowned Indian theologian, D. S. Amalorpavadass, has writ-ten eloquently on the role of consciousness/awareness in attaining spiritual integration and interiorization. He notes: "If wholeness is a state of being at which one should finally arrive in stages, awareness is the running thread and unifying force. Awareness needs to flow like a river, like a bloodstream.... Awareness is also the core of spirituality and God-experience."

"Awareness or consciousness should flow through the various actions of our life. One should maintain awareness in all that one does. It should serve as a running thread and connecting bond... through the various activities of our day, and the different periods and stages of our life in an uninterrupted and continuous flow. This flow will make our whole life a continuous prayer and a state of contemplation" (Amalorpavadass, 4, 24).

Brief glimpses at Scripture, Eastern traditions, a Trappist monk, and a contemporary theologian have shown that "consciousness" is a fruitful category to grasp the human-divine dynamic operative in the

Christian life. Within this framework – which is foundational – a vibrant spirituality and a concomitant missionary dynamism can flourish. And, in a Marian spirit, Christians who are missionary will grow ever more conscious of the marvelous deeds that God is accomplishing in us, our neighbors, our society, our church and the entire world.

THE CONSCIOUSNESS OF PAUL THE MISSIONARY

The New Testament describes the radical nature of Paul's awareness of God's active presence in his life. Though not naturally prone to humility, Paul admits that he was knocked to the ground (Acts 9:4) and that in Damascus "something like scales fell from his eyes" (Acts 9:18). His grace-filled conversion allowed him to perceive that he was the chosen instrument to bring Good News to the Gentiles and that he would accomplish his mission only with hardship and through suffering (Acts 9:15-16).

Paul's consciousness of his apostolic calling was certainly at the basis of his extraordinary missionary journeys. Without a vivid perception and faith commitment, no one would willingly endure the challenges Paul faced (II Cor. 11:23-30). Such endurance under trial would be no more than absolute foolishness! Yet, Paul is never willing – even momentarily – to minimize his authority and commitment as an apostle; the introductory verses of many of his letters are clear evidence of this fact. Paul's conversion was no superficial or passing phenomenon; it penetrated the core of his person and totally transformed his way of thinking and acting – his consciousness.

Further investigation into Pauline theology and spirituality reveals the depth of his convictions (RM 24). Paul is absolutely certain that God has a wonderful, marvelous, loving plan of salvation for the entire world (note his frequent use of the words *"mysterion"* and *"oikonomia"*). His letter to the Ephesians convincingly – almost mystically – explains how "God has given us the wisdom to understand fully the mystery" (1:9), "the mysterious design which for ages was hidden in God" (3:9).

Pauline reflection on God's loving plan of salvation *(mysterion)* synthesizes his belief that this design has been fully revealed in Christ the Savior and will be recapitulated in Christ at the end of time. This manifestation is focused on salvation, not condemnation or judgment, and is open to all peoples. It unfolds in stages: God, Jesus, Spirit, church, world; humanity's response is faith or personal appropriation of the *mysterion*.

A recent scholarly investigation (Plevnik, 477-478) has concluded that "Any center of Pauline theology must therefore include *all* these components of the apostle's gospel: his understanding of Christ and of God, his understanding of God's salvific action through Christ, involving the Easter event and its implications, the present lordship, the future coming of Christ, and the appropriation of salvation. The center is thus not any *single* aspect of Christ, or of God's action through Christ, but rather the whole and undivided richness and mystery of Christ and of the Father's saving purpose through his Son" *(mysterion)*. In brief, mystery could be a one-word synonym which captures the heart of the Christian message (RM 4, 44, 88).

Paul is the missionary *par excellence* because he believed, lived, prayed, served, reflected, witnessed, preached and suffered so that God's *mysterion* would be known, extended, loved and freely received. Obviously, Paul's missionary consciousness had the "*mysterion*-encounter" as its central focus and driving force.

Paul's self-awareness as an apostle was rooted in being chosen as a servant and minister of God's loving plan of salvation (Rom. 1:1-6; I Cor. 4:1; 15:9-11; Eph. 3:1-21; Col. 1:24-29). It might be asserted that the mysterion engulfed and consumed Paul; his consciousness was so transformed that he could assert that Christ lived in him (Gal. 2:20), that fellow-Christians could imitate him (I Cor. 4:16), that life or death no longer mattered (Rom. 14:8), and that he gloried in giving his life for Christ (II Tim. 4:6). In a word, the *mysterion* is foundational to Paul's missionary identity and consciousness!

MISSION AND *MYSTERION* CONSCIOUSNESS

The Second Vatican Council in its decree on the missionary activity of the church places mission and evangelization at the center of the church – not allowing this task to float somewhere on the periphery: "The pilgrim church is missionary by her very nature" (AG 2). Pope Paul VI continues in the same vein: "We wish to confirm once more that the task of evangelizing all peoples constitutes the essential mission of the church. . . . Evangelizing is in fact the grace and vocation proper to the church, her deepest identity. She exists in order to evangelize... " (EN

14). In his missionary encyclical Pope John Paul II seeks to give fresh impetus to missionary activity because it "is not considered a marginal task for the Church but is situated at the center of her life, as a fundamental commitment of the whole People of God" (RM 32; cf. RM 1, 40, 63).

To evangelize: what meaning does this imperative have for the church? It is to be no less than the living proclamation of the *mysterion* – God's loving design of universal salvation. As the community of Jesus' disciples, the church realizes her "deepest identity" and "her very nature" when she fulfills her mission of evangelization. She is to be always and everywhere "the universal sacrament of salvation" (LG 48; AG 1). For her, to live is to evangelize!

Phrased in contemporary language, the church accomplishes her "self-realization" or "self-actualization" through mission and evangelization. She is only authentic and true to herself when she is announcing and witnessing the *mysterion*. A non-missionary church is impossible; it is self-contradictory. Once again, the great missionary pope, Paul VI, writes that the church "is linked to evangelization in her most intimate being" (EN 15); mission is *not* "an optional contribution for the church" (EN 5). Quoting Vatican II (AG 29), Pope John Paul II reaffirms that missionary activity is "the greatest and holiest duty of the Church" (RM 63).

In addition, the church's missionary identity is not a late afterthought of the risen Jesus – though this outlook may seem true today of some Christians and local churches. Animation and rededication are necessary, because Christians "are faithful to the nature of the church to the degree that we love and sincerely promote her missionary activity" (EE 2).

These few paragraphs may invite the comment that "I've heard it all before." True, yet all of us often hear without hearing, see without seeing, and listen without comprehending (Mk 8:17-18). It is precisely at this juncture that the phenomenon of consciousness is poignantly relevant. Many Christians do not deny the missionary nature of the church, but their level of conscious awareness is weak or minimal. This fact is unfortunately true even of many full-time church personnel. The intention here is NOT to berate or castigate individuals; rather, it is a stark statement of the need for "consciousness-raising;" it is a call for Christians to expand and deepen their awareness; all urgently need "conscientization-into-mission." In short, the entire Church herself must experience a profound re-evangelization in order to become a truly evangelizing community (EN 13, 24; RM 47).

Recall some of the key themes presented earlier on the centrality of consciousness in Christian life and spirituality. In a unique way they seem particularly relevant as the Church struggles with her fundamental missionary identity. Is not this a central burning question in the Church today: What has happened to her mission consciousness – where is its urgency and dynamism – where are the contemporary St. Pauls?

A rephrasing in mission terms of earlier quotes on consciousness from Amalorpavadass may prove enlightening: Church-as-mission is "the running thread and unifying force"; it "needs to flow like a river, like a blood-stream"; it is at "the core of spirituality and God-experience"; it "will make our whole life a continuous prayer and state of contemplation."

TRINITARIAN FOUNDATIONS FOR MISSION CONSCIOUSNESS AND SPIRITUALITY

In the very same breath that the Vatican Council spoke of the church's missionary identity, it also presented the foundational rationale of mission. In a word, the *Why* of Church-as-Mission is Trinitarian: "For it is from the mission of the Son and the mission of the Holy Spirit that she takes her origin, in accordance with the decree of God the Father" (AG 2; cf. RM 1, 4, 32, 46).

This mission vision – expressed in Trinitarian language – must not frighten or intimidate readers. Do not say: "I don't understand Trinitarian theology, so I can't grasp this"! While a bit difficult and challenging, this insight is also beautiful and rewarding. It transports us to the heart of mission; it flows from the core of our faith in the Trinity; it greatly enhances our mission-consciousness and spirituality.

The most inviting manner to appreciate mission – via the Trinity – is to remember that it is an eminently *personal approach*. The Father is a person, his son Jesus is a person, their gift of the Spirit is also a person. This is only a statement of a basic dogma of the faith. Grasping this immanence/closeness of the three persons appears far more fruitful than grappling with the incomprehensibility of the transcendent Trinity.

Growth in consciousness-awareness-experience-encounter with each of the three persons richly broadens our vision of mission. It also manifests that mission theology and spirituality draw from the same wellspring. An appreciation of the roles of the Father, the Son, and the Spirit in mission produces an integrated missiology, incorporating "Abba"-theology, Christology, and Pneumatology. The result will certainly be a more holistic theology-spirituality of mission.

Finally, it is the firm conviction of this author that such an approach serves to relieve some current tensions and questions in mission. For example, debates centered on interreligious dialogue with the living faith traditions of the world can probably be better resolved more from a Pneumatological approach than from only a Christological viewpoint. Therefore, if mission theology and spirituality are an integrated endeavor, the deepened consciousness will provide insights to approach both theoretical and practical questions.

Our attention now turns to the unique roles of Father, Son, and Spirit in mission. The goal of this discussion is a heightened awareness of how each person of the Trinity sends and accompanies us into mission. Recall the title of this presentation which links mission and spirituality with a consciousness of being sent (cf. RM 88).

THE ROLE OF THE FATHER

The Father is presented in Scripture as the harvest master and vineyard owner (Mt. 20:1-16; 21:33-43). Mission, therefore, originates with the Father; mission is *God's project* (RM 12-13, 24). The Father determines its parameters. Already this awareness places the church and her evangelizers in an auxiliary, servant role.

Vatican II clearly set aside triumphalistic ecclesiology as well as any simplistic church-kingdom identification. As servant of the kingdom or laborer in the vineyard, the Church is to be "the kingdom of Christ now present in mystery" and "the initial budding forth of that kingdom" (LG 3, 5). In addition, the Council, situating the Church within the larger framework of God's design of salvation *(mysterion)*, entitled its first chapter of the Dogmatic Constitution on the Church: "The Mystery of the Church." Within this context, the Church and all missioners must radically see themselves serving the *mysterion*, "according to the will of God the Father" (AG 2).

Truly, the Father desires *generous cooperators* and humble workers for the harvest (Mt. 20:1-16; Lk. 10:1-11). He freely chooses them and they are to belong to him (Lk. 6:13; Mk. 3:13-16); Jn. 15:15-16). These passages remind evangelizers that all mission is a sending *(missio/mittere)*, originating in the Father; their vocation is God's gratuitous gift. Missioners do not send themselves; mission cannot be defined in legal terms; all must be according to the Father's gracious design. Affirming mission, therefore, as a gratuitous gift in the Father's gracious vision, emphasizes the centrality of grace. Thus, missioners understand, as the country priest in Bernanos' novel says on his deathbed, in all vocations "Grace is everywhere" (Bernanos, 233).

Trinitarian mission is always soteriological; its purpose is *liberation and salvation*. The Father has no other goal as Paul clearly reminded Timothy: he "wants all to be saved and come to know the truth" (I Tim. 2:4). Condemnation or rejection are inconsistent with the Father's design (Jn. 3:16-17; Mt. 18:14). The Father, overwhelmingly "rich in mercy" (Eph. 2:4; RM 12), extends his great love to everyone as the *universalism* of both Luke and Paul portray.

All evangelizers have experienced "the kindness and love of God" (Tit. 3:4); it is out of their deep consciousness of the Father's personal graciousness that they journey to all places, peoples, and cultures. They are aware that they have received all as gift and they desire to give all with the same generosity (Mt. 10:8). Any missioner would relish being described as being "rich in mercy"!

The Father cannot be surpassed in his kindness and generosity (Jas. 1:5; 1:17); his mercy is made concrete and visible when he sends Jesus his son. This is definitely a new mode of God's presence with his people – it is love in *personal form*. This unfolding of the *mysterion* far surpasses previous manifestations of Yahweh's presence to his people Israel (Heb. 1:1-2). Missioners strive to be continuations of the love of God manifested personally in Jesus – and this approach brings transformation and deepened consciousness.

Our discussion of the Father's role in mission carries us back to the heart of the Trinity. God is fundamentally love (I Jn. 4:8) and all manifestations flow from this identity. No less than the inner life of the Trinity is founded on the dynamism of divine love. Thus, the *mysterion* necessarily is a *loving design* since it arises "from that 'fountain of love' or charity *(fontalis amor)* within God the Father" (AG 2).

It is imperative that missioners and evangelizers become mystics like John the Evangelist (cf. I Jn. 4:7-21); nothing less can explain the love of God for a fallen world and rebellious humanity (RM 5). No other motivation is adequate to the missionary calling – of the entire church! Mother Teresa of Calcutta has named her congregation the Missionaries of Charity and she never tires of reminding her audiences that this is the fundamental vocation of all Christians. It sounds fantastic – but it is true: the love of the Trinity is personally poured into our hearts and it transforms all evangelizers into missionary messengers of God's limitless love! Knowing our personal God as the font of love is the highest level of consciousness possible. Mission spirituality becomes a conscious centering on Trinitarian love. This is the solid missiology-become-spirituality promoted by Vatican II.

THE MISSION OF THE SON

Jesus declares openly that he has been sent by his loving Father; precisely, the phrase "the Father who sent me" occurs 46 times in the Gospel of John. And, a salvific thrust is evident in the missioning of Jesus by his Father. Vatican II expresses Jesus' mission as a *reconciling presence*: "...to establish peace or communion between sinful human beings and Himself... Jesus Christ was sent into the world as a real Mediator between God and men" (AG 3). In Paul's theology, mediation and reconciliation are vital elements of the *mysterion* (II Cor. 5:19; Col. 1:13; Rom. 5:1).

Jesus' continuing *"Abba-experience"* (Kavunkal, 9-15) – enabling him to faithfully accomplish his mission – has several dimensions: his coming or proceeding from the Father (noted above), his remaining with the Father (Jn. 10:38; 16:32), and his eventual return to the Father (Jn. 16:5; 7:33; 13:36). This means that Jesus fulfills his mission in light of a particular consciousness: continual intimacy with his Father. Luke tells us that before making such a decisive move in his ministry as the choice of the Twelve, Jesus "went out to the mountains to pray, spending the night in communion with God (Lk. 6:12). Mission in the Jesus mode has its source, continuation, and fulfillment in the "Abba-experience." This dimension in Jesus' pattern of living mission provides evangelizers an inviting model for their own mission consciousness (cf. RM 4-11).

In its holistic vision of God's design for salvation, the Council sees the church as continuing, developing, and unfolding "the mission of Christ Himself" (AG 5). The apostolic exhortation *Evangelii Nuntiandi* (13-16, 59-60), the pastoral statement on world mission of the United States Bishops *To the Ends of the Earth* (25-27), and the mission encyclical *Redemptoris Missio* (9) all confirm mission as an ecclesial act in fidelity to Jesus.

Contemporary evangelizers, cognizant of the Jesus-Church continuity, seek to live and witness as the community of Jesus' followers. They recall his promises (Mt. 16:18; 28:20), but readily admit they are fragile "earthen vessels" (II Cor. 4:7). They faithfully accept that "Christ in His mission from the Father is the fountain and source of the whole apostolate of the Church" (AA 4). A missioner's model is *"sentire cum ecclesia"* (feel and think with the church), frankly admitting that one is *"simul justus et peccator"* (concomitantly both upright and sinful). Who among Jesus' followers does not need a deeper consciousness of these realities?

Central to the mission of Jesus is the mystery of the Incarnation: "the Son of God walked the ways of a true Incarnation that He might make men sharers in the divine nature" (AG 3). This radical identification of our brother Jesus with us mortals (Heb. 4:15) makes us rich out of his poverty (II Cor. 8:9). He became a servant (Mk. 10:45) and gave his life "as a ransom for the many – that is, for all" (AG 3).

Consistently, Church Fathers of both East and West have held that "what was not taken up [assumed] by Christ was not healed" (Abbott, 587: note 9). Thus, when Jesus took to himself our entire humanity, he healed, renewed, and saved us. In brief, Incarnation is the fundamental pattern of all mission. Today evangelizers are deeply conscious of the ramifications of *mission as incarnation*. No missioner worthy of the name underestimates the importance of indigenization and inculturation; they develop a spirituality of "depth identification," becoming as vulnerable as Jesus was in his humanity. This same pattern is the model of growth and development of all local churches (AG 22; RM 52-54).

While it is certain that the mission of Jesus is initiated at the Incarnation, his baptism by John in the Jordan is an act of *public commitment-consecration to mission*. Jesus pursues his ministry; though it will encounter growing opposition and lead to the human disaster of Calvary, he will not betray his commitment (RM 88).

Note that Matthew, Mark, and Luke all juxtapose Jesus' baptism and the triple temptations in the wilderness. The tactic of Satan is to subvert Jesus with possessions, pride, and power; at the core, all Satan's promises tantalize Jesus to renege on his dedication to mission. The more conscious that an evangelizer becomes of the struggle involved in mission-faithfulness, the closer he will be drawn to Jesus "who in every respect has been tempted as we are, yet without sin." The missioner will constantly and with confidence "approach the throne of grace to receive mercy and favor and to find help in time of need" (Heb. 4:15-16).

Instructive for the Church and her evangelizers is an appreciation of the *continual action of the Spirit in the life of Jesus*. The creed affirms that he was conceived "by the power of the Holy Spirit." The same Spirit descends on Jesus at the moment of his baptism (Mt. 3:17); he is led by the Spirit to the desert (Mt. 4:1); he returns to Galilee in the power of the Spirit (Lk. 4:14); he begins his preaching mission at Nazareth asserting that "the Spirit of the Lord is upon me" (Lk. 4:18).

As Jesus was empowered by the Spirit, he sends forth his own disciples saying: "Receive the Holy Spirit" (Jn. 20:22). Peter (Acts 4:8), Paul (Acts 9:17), and Stephen (Acts 6:5; 7:55), as well as those who listened to their preaching (Acts 10:44), were all filled with the Spirit. In fact, the entire nascent Church brims with the Spirit's presence (Acts 2:4) and thus, the community increases while it enjoys the consolation of the befriending Spirit (Acts 9:31). Jesus, his disciples, and likewise today's evangelizers all are in mission through the marvelous action of the Spirit (Kroeger-A, 3-12; RM 87).

Concretely in the practical order, Jesus carries out his *mission through evangelization* – proclaiming the Good News of the Kingdom. The first words that Mark places on Jesus' lips are centered on this very theme (Mk. 1:15). Luke also portrays Jesus' mission as focused on glad tidings to the "little ones of this world" (Lk. 4:18-19). As Paul VI has noted, this theme "sums up the whole mission of Jesus" (EN 6). Jesus could not be impeded in his ministry: "I must announce the good news of the reign of God, because that is why I was sent" (Lk. 4:43; RM 22).

Contemporary evangelizers, reflecting on the urgency and scope of Jesus' kingdom proclamation, will find themselves imitating Jesus' ministry as he lived it in silence, in action, in dialogue, in teaching, and in prayer. Yes, the Good News of the Kingdom for Jesus means an integral, holistic approach to evangelization – because all dimensions of the total gospel are expressions of his enduring love (Jn. 13:1; cf. RM 11, 20, 24-36, 41-60, 83).

Jesus' entire life, from the Incarnation to Pentecost, was a proclamation. All he said and did were a testimony to the Father's loving design (Jn. 3:31-35; 7:16; 8:38; 14:24). Jesus existed on nothing else; his "sustenance-food-meat" was to do the will and work of the one who sent him (Jn. 4:34). In everything Jesus was faithful to the Father.

Reflective, insightful evangelizers interiorize the *fidelity mind-set of Jesus* (Phil. 2:5); they also imitate St. Paul in his concern for faithful transmission of the message of Jesus preserved by the church (I Cor. 15:3, 11). In prayer and meditation missioners re-focus themselves on Jesus and his kingdom – and often this demands setting aside personal opinions and ambitions. Mother Teresa of Calcutta notes that Jesus does not always call us to be successful, but he always invites us to be faithful.

This fidelity to Jesus and his message should not be interpreted in too narrow a sense. As announcers of Good News, we consciously interiorize Jesus' Gospel values; however, we seek to transmit them to humanity in all its cultural, social, religious, and politico-economic diversity (RM 28-29). Certainly, this is a fantastic challenge; it is central to contemporary evangelization. Paul VI expressed it so wisely and so poignantly: "This fidelity both to a message whose servants we are and to the people to whom we must transmit it living and intact is the central axis of evangelization" (EN 4).

Life-style – certainly a key focal-point in any vision of evangelization. For our contemporaries, who only willingly listen to witnesses (rather than theoreticians), the missioner's authenticity and transparency are generally the first elements in evangelization; wordless witness is already a silent, powerful, and effective proclamation. It is an initial act of evangelization (EN 21, 41; RM 42-43, 59).

Jesus himself adopted a particular, concrete life-style. His mind-set was of fidelity and obedience to his Father; his outward manner manifested the lived values of poverty, total dedication, persecution, apparent failure. The Church and her evangelizers "must walk the same road which Christ walked: a road of poverty and obedience, of service and self-sacrifice to the death" (AG 5; cf. RM 90-91).

Bluntly, there is no authentic Christian mission without the cross – and all its surprises, foolishness, and scandal (I Cor. 1:18-25). True mission is *always signed by the cross*, and without it we cannot be Jesus disciples. The evangelizer is always generous in bearing a personal share of the hardships which the gospel entails (II Tim. 1:8). Constantly, the Christian disciple is measuring one's life and apostolate against the life-style of Jesus and the patterns of the gospel. Sustained prayerful reflection and an ever-deepening consciousness of one's personal relationship with the Trinity are the unique way of interiorizing the paradox of the cross – and the power of the resurrection.

An anonymous poet, speaking of the centrality of the Incarnation and Redemption in Christianity, noted that there are no definitions in God's dictionary for these terms. One must search for the meaning of Bethlehem and Calvary under another category. Their significance is to be found only when one reads how God defines *love*!

Indeed, God's loving plan of salvation is a message of hope for all peoples. It is universal and should be preached/witnessed "to the ends of the earth" (Mt. 28:18-19a; Mk. 16:15; Lk. 24:47). To spread this *universal message* demands great dedication and faith as seen in the practical advice that Paul gave to Timothy (II Tim. 4:1-5).

The evangelizer, conscious of one's role in the actualization of the *mysterion*, will surrender enthusiastically to the invitation of Jesus: Come and follow me in my mission. This conscious surrender will open the disciple's eyes to perceive, not so much what individual efforts are accomplishing, but how God-Father-Son-Spirit are working fruitfully in and through one's life. With this vision, contemplation and action harmoniously blend and sustain one another; the evangelizer experiences living the *mysterion*. Eventually, all will be *recapitulated in Christ* and God will be all in all (I Cor. 15:24-28).

This lengthy section on the mission of Jesus can fittingly be concluded by recalling Paul's reminder to the Corinthians: "Look, I am telling you a mystery" (I Cor. 15:51). This same *mysterion*-awareness is central in the evangelizer's consciousness; energized by it, one readily accepts Paul's encouragement: "Be steadfast and persevering, my beloved brothers, fully engaged in the work of the Lord. You know that your toil is not in vain when it is done in the Lord" (I Cor. 15:58).

THE MISSION OF THE HOLY SPIRIT

"Evangelization will never be possible without the action of the Holy Spirit... the Holy Spirit is the principal agent of evangelization" (EN 75;

cf. RM 21, 30). Clearer words cannot be found to describe the *centrality of the Spirit's action* in the life of the Church and her evangelizers. This activity has a continuity; it is present as the Spirit fills the life of Jesus, the Church, missioner-apostles, the entire laity. Essential for all – and no one can claim a monopoly on the Spirit who "blows where he wills" (Jn. 3:8).

Luke's Gospel puts the action of the Spirit at the beginning (4:18) and end (24:49) of Jesus' ministry; similarly, in the Acts of the Apostles (often popularly known as "the Gospel of the Holy Spirit"), Luke also places the Spirit's action at the beginning of the Church (1:8), throughout its early expansion, and within the final address of Paul (28:25). Mission continually demands the life-giving presence and action of the Spirit (Kroeger-B, 449-455; RM 24).

Though generally weak in its appreciation of pneumatology, the Church now lives in a time of rediscovery, especially in Vatican II, the 1974 Synod on Evangelization, and the 1986 encyclical *Dominum et Vivificantem* of John Paul II. All evangelizers need a similar growth in consciousness, affirming the Spirit's accompaniment at every moment in mission; all mission is *"a sending forth in the Spirit"* (RM 22). It is imperative that this consciousness focus on the personal presence of the Spirit – whom John Paul II calls "Person-love" and "Person-gift" (DV 10, 22, 50).

Concomitant with accepting the Spirit as "the principal agent of evangelization," missioners collaborate closely with him; they are *"team-mates"* in the work of evangelization. This continual dialogue reveals the full truth of Jesus' teaching and person (Jn. 16:13-15). The insights perceived are uniquely apropos to the context and challenges emerging within the evangelizer's apostolate. Progress in everything (e.g. indigenization of theology, liturgy, church organization; social justice ministry; international solidarity, etc.) depends upon an in-depth personal-communal discernment of the Spirit's promptings. It is the Spirit who opens hearts and moves people. Apostolic fruitfulness does not depend on one's own ingenuity or organizational ability – but upon the power of the Spirit and the Risen Lord Jesus (RM 23).

St. Paul intimately knew the workings of Jesus and the Spirit in his life. A particularly revealing passage describes Paul's experience in Asia Minor (Acts 16:6-10; cf. RM 21). Twice it is noted that they "had been prevented by the Holy Spirit," that "the Spirit of Jesus would not allow them" to enter certain provinces. Modern-day Pauls also need a *"theol-*

ogy of road-blocks," because not all their plans and projects will meet acceptance or success. Evangelizers may dream that their cooperation with the Spirit will always produce glowing results; however, this would not be living in reality. Only the ongoing interpersonal dialogue between evangelizer and Spirit in reflective prayer will enlighten one to see the detours and road-blocks as a form of the Spirit's guiding presence.

Such faith-consciousness provides the *equilibrium* missioners need in facing a wide diversity of challenges; it gives insight on how to "let go and let God"; it aids the apostle in avoiding the traps of bitterness, cynicism, depression and contemporary burn-out. The Spirit will reveal how the cross of Jesus is a yoke that is easy and a burden that is light (Mt. 11:28-30). Evangelizers will develop a spirituality of optimism, hope, and confidence – knowing that they can readily count on the strength of the Spirit.

This discussion of various aspects of the Spirit's role in mission should always be placed within the *inclusive framework* of the *mysterion* – that loving plan of God for humanity's salvation. Then, for example, with the awareness that mission is God's project, our frustrations and difficulties can be integrated into a faithful surrender to God's wisdom. This same inclusive view of the *mysterion* is essential to perceive the Spirit's role in interfaith or interreligious dialogue (RM 55-57).

Evangelizers need to be cognizant of the Church's own growth-in-consciousness in recent years on the Spirit-religions dynamic (Kroeger-D). Vatican II spoke positively of the Spirit's diverse activity in the world (GS 38); the 1974 Synod on Evangelization affirmed "the Holy Spirit's action which overflows the bounds of the Christian community" (EMW 11). John Paul II in two encyclicals has spoken of the "effects of the Spirit of truth operating outside the visible confines of the Mystical Body" (RH 6) and of the need to appreciate "the Holy Spirit's activity also 'outside the visible body of the Church'" (DV 53; cf. RM 28-29).

Perhaps it is not an overstatement to assert that *"Spirit-consciousness"* is uniquely necessary for all evangelizers – particularly in the Asian context. Only the Spirit can foster the awareness and sensitivity needed to approach the diversity of Asian peoples, cultures, and religions. Many peoples are in poverty and underdevelopment, requiring deep social transformation; the cultures should find authentic religious expression within gospel-inculturation; religions and their followers must be treasured because, as the Asian bishops have noted, "we accept them as significant and positive elements in the economy of God's design of salvation" (FABC-I 14).

In light of these realities, the missioner's daily communing with the Spirit will foster *renewal and conversion* (as an opening to a deeper God-consciousness). It will enhance one's vision to see the active presence of the Spirit in peoples, cultures, and religions – both within and beyond the Christian community. The Spirit will provide the sensitive balance in both "bringing" God's love and Kingdom values and in "discovering" their presence already operative. The Spirit's diverse gifts (charisms) will generously be directed to their proper, fruitful employment. The apostle of Jesus is that person who is possessed by the Spirit – and is deeply conscious of it!

The evangelizer's heightened awareness of the Spirit's role in one's life is not somehow only a narcissistic or individualistic awareness. It is to be fully integrated within *the community*, within the local Church. Constantly there is openness and sensitivity to what the Spirit is saying to the Churches and how they must "grow in missionary consciousness, fervor, commitment and zeal" (EN 58; cf. RM 86).

In contemporary approaches to evangelization, this attention to the guiding Spirit within the *local Church* is a crucial imperative. It has been noted that the book of Revelation specifically mentions the names and places of the seven churches, concluding all the admonitions with exactly the same words: "Let him who has ears heed the Spirit's word to the Churches (Rev. 2:7, 11, 17, 29; 3:6, 13, 22). Thus, taking its cue from Pauline ecclesiology and based on the insights of Vatican II (LG 23; AG 19-22), all current missiology-spirituality gives due consideration to the voice of local Churches empowered through the Spirit (RM 48-50).

The Asian bishops repeatedly affirm that the "primary focus of our task of evangelization then, at this time in our history, is the building up of a truly local church... the local church is a church incarnate in a people... this means concretely a church in continuous, humble and loving dialogue with the living traditions, the cultures, the religions. . ." (FABC-I 9, 12). A pivotal document of the universal Church affirms the same stance: "Every local church is responsible for the totality of mission" (D&M 14).

Evangelizers – indigenous and expatriate – in harmonious interaction with the local Church are always conscious of the personal Spirit maintaining them in mission. What is *the source* of their optimism, courage, unity, patience, detachment-poverty – even martyrdom (Rom.

15:18-19; Heb. 2:3-4)? Who inspires them to bring forth enduring fruit
and convincing witness (Jn. 15:16; Gal. 5:22-23)? Who "causes people
to discern the signs of the times – signs willed by God" (EN 75; Kroeger-
C)? All these gifts surely have as their source "the love of God that has
been poured out in our hearts through the Holy Spirit who has been
given to us (Rom. 5:5). To every evangelizer the Spirit is indeed "Person-
love" and "Person-gift."

CONCLUDING SYNTHESIS

The author of this piece remains totally cognizant that a contemplative-
mystical thread spans this entire presentation; it has focused on "consciousness of the *mysterion*" as foundational to a spirituality of the
apostolate. This emphasis, of course, is in harmony with the central
missiological insight of Vatican II: the Trinitarian foundation of mission
(AG 2-4).

This perspective resonates well with what the Spirit is saying to all
the Churches – particularly in Asia. It is noteworthy that the First Plenary
Assembly of the Federation of Asian Bishops' Conferences – FABC I
(Taipei, 1974) discussed "Evangelization and Modern Day Asia." Signifi-
cantly, the next Plenary Assembly – FABC II (Barrackpore-Calcutta,
1978), designed to be in harmonious continuity with the challenges of
evangelization discussed in FABC I, focused on "Prayer – the Life of the
Church in Asia."

Evangelization and Prayer, Missiology and Spirituality: these are
two coordinates of one integral process (cf. RM 78). All evangelizers
seek to enhance their consciousness of the intimate personal activity of
the triune God within their lives, attitudes, values, and activities. Thus,
witness of life, faith- consciousness, and diverse forms of evangelization
coalesce into an integrated unity.

Permit a brief return to the statement of FABC-II on prayer and a
spirituality for evangelization. The Asian bishops affirm the need for
"conscious personal communion with God our Father, in Christ Jesus.
It is the fruit of the Holy Spirit working in our hearts." They note that
"the spirituality characteristic of the religions of our continent stresses
a deeper awareness of God and the whole self in recollection, silence
and prayer, flowering in openness to others, in compassion, non-
violence, generosity." They sincerely desire "a genuine renewal and

revitalization of these realities in our prayer-life" (FABC-II 14, 35, 20). This, in short, is the "Asian formula" for mission spirituality!

This presentation has been a long pilgrimage toward an holistic view of missiology-spirituality. The sign-posts on the road have indicated the need of awareness, Pauline theology, "*mysterion*-consciousness," Trinitarian foundations, and the personal role of Father, Son, and Spirit in the lives of all evangelizers. The ground that has been traversed has included the two-fold journey of all missioners: the inward journey of deepened consciousness or spirituality which overflows during the outward journey of all evangelizing endeavors.

And yet, much more needs to be explored – at another sitting (cf: Kroeger-E). This cursory treatment of diverse yet complementary elements of mission spirituality plunges the reader into an acceptance of the fact that no eye has seen, no ear has heard, no mind has conceived what God has prepared for those who love him (I Cor. 2:9).

If I were tasked to summarize the core insight into mission and spirituality required by all evangelizers, I would readily and confidently respond by affirming: You and I all need a vibrant, conscious awareness that *we are sent* – by the love of the Father, the grace of Jesus, and the power of the Spirit. This insight fired St. Paul in both his theology and missionary activity – it will do no less for contemporary apostles. Missioners, following St. Therese of Lisieux the patroness of mission, are people conscious that they are on fire with the love of God; they know they have been sent to light a fire on the earth (Lk. 12:49); how they wish the blaze were ignited!

BIBLIOGRAPHY CITED IN THIS CHAPTER

Abbott, W. (Editor). *The Documents of Vatican II.* London: Geoffrey Chapman, 1966.

Amalorpavadass, D. S. "Priestly Formation: Integration and Interiorization": A paper presented at the First Joint Colloquium of Rectors and Spiritual Directors of Asian Seminaries. Sponsored by: Federation of Asian Bishops' Conferences: February 9-15, 1990; Canossa House of Spirituality; Tagaytay City, Philippines.

Bernanos, G. *The Diary of a Country Priest.* Garden City, New York: Image Books, 1974.

Higgins, J. *Thomas Merton on Prayer*. Garden City, New York: Image Books, 1975.

Kavunkal, J. "The 'Abba Experience' of Jesus: The Model and Motive for Mission Today," In: *FABC Papers Number 43*. Hong Kong: Federation of Asian Bishops' Conferences, 1986; pp. 9-15.

Kroeger, J. A "The Foundational Role of the Spirit in Mission," *Maryknoll Formation Journal* Vol. 6, No. 2 (Summer, 1987), pp. 3-12.

_____. B "Mission – Led by the Spirit," *Review for Religious* Vol. 47, No. 3 (May-June, 1988), pp. 449-455. Reprinted in: *Omnis Terra* (English) Vol. 23, No. 197 (April, 1989), pp. 224-228; *Omnis Terra* (Spanish) Vol. 21, No. 190 (April, 1989), pp. 219-224.

_____. C " 'Signs of the Times': A Thirty-year Panorama," *East Asian Pastoral Review* Vol. 26, No. 2 (1989), pp. 191-196.

_____. D (Editor). *Interreligious Dialogue: Catholic Perspectives*. Davao City, Philippines: Mission Studies Institute, 1990.

_____. E *Mission Today*. Hong Kong: Federation of Asian Bishops' Conferences, 1991.

Merton, T. A *Spiritual Direction and Meditation*. Collegeville: The Liturgical Press, 1960.

_____. B *Faith and Violence*. Notre Dame: University of Notre Dame Press, 1968.

Plevnik, J. "The Center of Pauline Theology," *The Catholic Biblical Quarterly* Vol. 51, No. 3 (July, 1989), pp. 461-478.

God's Universal Rainbow Covenant

The year 2000 is rapidly approaching. Some startling statistics – fantastic figures – confront the Christian Church. One notes a few examples: all Christians together will be 34% of the world's population, numbering only twice as many as the total number of nonreligious/nonbelievers; there will be more Muslims than Roman Catholics on the globe when the third millennium arrives; well over one-half of humanity lives in Asia, where the dominant religions are Buddhism, Islam, and Hinduism. These realities impinge forcefully on Christian consciousness, and modern communications serve to highlight the vast pluriformity of peoples, cultures, religions, and traditions.

How can contemporary theology and scriptural interpretation sensitively meet the world religions and peoples of these living faiths? Can Christians avoid prejudicial, antagonistic, and exclusivist modes of thinking and expression? Is it possible to maintain a double fidelity to the biblical message and also to the peoples of diverse religions? How are bridges to be built between biblical theology and the world's living faith traditions?

INTERPRETATION OF THE HEBREW SCRIPTURES (OLD TESTAMENT) AND UNIVERSALISM

Contemporary Scripture interpretation remains receptive to a broad understanding of God's action within history and human events. This is based on the recognition of God's twofold intervention: [a] a universal commitment to all peoples; and [b] a particular commitment to the Israelites. If one explicitly focuses on the biblical universalism of the Hebrew scriptures, many themes emerge showing God's global action: the goodness of creation, the universal providence of God, and the wisdom shared by all peoples. In addition, by concentrating on the covenant theme, specifically the universal covenant with Noah in the ninth chapter of Genesis, one can glean further insights toward reading Scripture with a sensitivity to the followers of other great world religions.

God's rainbow covenant with Noah is set within the first eleven chapters of Genesis, which describe primeval history, the origin of the world and the human race. These chapters form a type of preface to the entire Bible, giving it a universalistic orientation. In addition, they serve to demonstrate that even prior to the revelation to Abraham, Yahweh is revealed as Lord of the entire universe. Also, the covenant with Noah is a concrete example of God's universal love (cf. RM 12).

Surprisingly, the Noachic covenant is portrayed as the oldest of all covenants. It is promised in Genesis 6:18 and actualized in Genesis 9:17. It is contracted with Noah and his descendants: all people who will ever live. Evidently, its universal nature bespeaks God's commitment to all humanity's welfare and salvation. There is almost total agreement that this section is authored by the Pentateuchal Priestly writer (P). This theology, emerging from Israel's exilic period of contact with peoples of other religions, is often expressed through accounts about covenants. While emphasis on covenant is not exclusively found within P material, its presence does represent a key theological prism of the P tradition.

Covenant is an essential concept in any interpretation of Scripture. Its Hebrew word *berith* describes in various ways the relationship between God and humanity. One notes that in all of Genesis 1-11, there is a retrojected use of later covenant theology to describe the God-humanity bond which existed from the beginning of the world. In addition, it should be highlighted that in the promise of the covenant with Noah (Gen. 6:18), as well as in its enactment (Gen. 9, specifically verses 9, 11, 12, 13, 15, 16, 17), the precise word *berith* is used. Since this covenant is with all of the descendants of Noah, Israel cannot claim the exclusive privilege of being a covenanted people with God.

SCOPE OF THE COVENANT WITH NOAH

Further exploration reveals significant characteristics of the rainbow covenant. It is an agreement which is universalistic/comprehensive in its breadth. It is not simply a pact between two individuals, God and Noah. God contracts with Noah and with all his descendants (9:9). Noah represents the second father of humanity, and he even receives the same injunction which God had given Adam: "Be fruitful and multiply, and fill the earth" (Gen. 1:28, 9:1). It was from Noah and his wife and their descendants that "the whole earth was peopled" (9:19). God continues this intimate relationship with all peoples, extending divine grace freely to the whole human race. The Noachic covenant is to be everlasting (9:16), established for "all future generations" (9:12). This is a covenant permanent in its validity at every point in history. It is not merely a past event, but an ever-present faith reality. In the view of the Priestly author, God irrevocably extends divine grace and promises so that future dealings with all peoples will redound to their welfare and blessing.

Clearly, this covenant flows from divine initiative. Emphasis is repeatedly laid on God's active role: this is "*my* covenant with you" (9:11); "the covenant *I* make between *me* and you" (9:12); "the covenant between *me* and you" (9:15); "the covenant *I* have made (9:17). Surprisingly, Noah promises nothing and no demands are placed upon him. Unconditionally, absolutely and totally, God covenants with all life and particularly with all of humankind.

The sign of authentication of this universal and everlasting covenant is the rainbow: "my bow in the clouds." Verses 12, 13, and 17 all mention this sign of the covenant. As sign, it points beyond itself to God's sovereign activity on behalf of all people. It affirms that humanity's existence is blessed and will reach fulfillment in the loving plan of God. This bow is not a weapon of war. On the contrary, it is a sign of peace, a sign of God's pledge that "never again will all life be cut off..., never again will there be a flood to destroy the earth" (9:11).

Finally, as a consequence of the Noachic covenant, one finds the List of Nations in Genesis 10. The rainbow covenant is effective, and the earth is again filled with a multitude of nations. All these peoples are born from the blessings of God, each people with its own country, culture, and destiny. Their unity and diversity realize God's design inaugurated at creation and renewed after the flood. With remarkable creativity the Priestly author has enshrined this message in dignified covenant language: God is a sure hope for all peoples; God's dependability and love are everlasting within the economy of salvation!

THE RAINBOW COVENANT AND WORLD RELIGIONS

The most fundamental conclusion arising from an exploration of Genesis 9:1-17 affirms the universal saving action of God for all peoples. Indeed, this may be stating the obvious, but in the past this universal dimension of God's salvific design has been underemphasized within biblical theology. Ordinarily, the Exodus from Egypt or perhaps the call of Abraham have been the point of departure in preaching and catechesis. Thus, although there is strong universalism in the Abraham story, it could appear as if God called only the people Israel and became the tribal God of Abraham and Sarah, Isaac and Rebecca, and Jacob and Rachel and Leah. Unwittingly, the fact that God's revelation and grace are available for all peoples became clouded or underemphasized. All other peoples, as well as their religions, were simply viewed as belonging to non-Judaeo-Christian traditions. By neglecting a full elaboration of Genesis 1-11, an appreciation of the dignity of other peoples and their ways of life was never adequately promoted. Refocused scriptural theology can contribute to the correction of a certain unfortunate and false ethnocentrism within Judaism and Christianity.

This challenge demands a balancing act, an integration of Israel's election within God's universal design. The Pentateuchal tradition itself affirms both the universal and particular dimensions of God's saving design; the choice of Israel is not to be understood exclusively, but inclusively. On this point the book *God's Chosen Peoples* by W. Buhlmann (page 35) speaks eloquently on the mutual vocation of Israel and the nations:

> ... theological reflection... makes it clear that Israel's election occurred only and solely in view of the peoples, the gentiles. In the concrete case of the one people, all peoples were chosen.... Thus it was not because God had no care for other peoples that he chose Israel, but precisely *because* he cared for other peoples. Israel was not elected to a privilege but to a service: to reveal God's affection to all peoples.

An integrated reading of the Hebrew Scriptures (Old Testament) excludes any notion whatsoever of exclusive ethnic pride, superiority, or excessive nationalism. The election of Israel does not indicate any rejection of the nations. God's rainbow covenant establishes God's rule over all the nations on earth, Israel among them. It envisions mutuality, not false dichotomies such as Israel versus the nations, believers versus heathens, male versus female, colored versus white, North versus South.

Recall that this short piece bears the subtitle: "Relating Scripture with World Religions." Admittedly, one will search in vain for a full theology of other religious traditions either in the Hebrew or Christian Scriptures. What is found, however, are glimpses and orientations of a respectful attitude toward the followers of other living faiths. These elements, and the Noachic covenant is a prime example, can be used as biblical foundations for interreligious dialogue and human interaction. These same universalistic themes need emphasis by preachers and evangelizers, whether they be in a Christian, Muslim, Hindu, or Buddhist milieu; whether they live in the First, Second, or Third World. The human family needs continuous strengthening against forces which deny its unity and solidarity, forces such as war, racism, prejudice, exclusivistic nationalism, religious bigotry. The narrative of God's rainbow covenant with all humanity demands frequent retelling.

Finally, one might reflect upon an insight shared by most missionaries who have lengthy transcultural experience. They conclude that all peoples and nations perceive themselves as being a *chosen people*. Thus, there is the need that biblical faith be credibly proclaimed and lived so that all can link their own cultural and religious experience with the universal love that God has manifested in the Scriptures. Humankind in its ethnic diversity is inherently the beneficiary of the tenderness of God; all are covenanted people in that universal covenant the Lord has concluded with Noah.

5

Awakening to the Spirit

In one brief paragraph, the historic Second Vatican Council comprehensively summarized the foundations of mission: "The pilgrim Church is missionary by her very nature. For it is from the mission of the Son and the mission of the Holy Spirit that she takes her origin, in accordance with the decree of God the Father" (AG 2). In a word, mission emanates from the Trinitarian nature of God; this places missionary activity at the center of the Church's faith and life – no longer on its periphery (cf. EN 14; RM 1, 32, 40, 63).

In the quarter-century since the completion of Vatican II, mission theology has seen many developments of the Council's seminal concepts. Within this growth, there has been, among varied emphases, a deepened perception of the role of the Spirit as essential to a comprehensive theology of mission. Evangelization – its many approaches and emphases – seems naturally linked to a holistic pneumatology (theology of the Holy Spirit). Most dominant themes in contemporary missiology are clearly – even essentially – linked with an adequate appreciation of the Holy Spirit as the principal agent of evangelization (EN 75; RM 21, 30).

This panoramic presentation endeavors to present a capsulized description of some areas current within missiology – areas that link pneumatology and mission theology.

Mission today necessarily is understood within the new outlook and ecclesiology promoted by the event of Vatican II (1962-1965). What has emerged is a new vision of the Church and her mission, a new openness to the modern world, and a spirit of *aggiornamento* and self-renewal; all have been the work of the Spirit. Thus, before mentioning specific themes of the Council, one seeks to appreciate Vatican II itself as a unique manifestation of the Spirit: "this most sacred Synod... has been gathered in the Holy Spirit" (LG 1); "the Council brings to mankind light kindled... under the guidance of the Holy Spirit" (GS 3). More recently, John Paul II asserted that "the teaching of this Council is essentially 'pneumatological'; it is *permeated by the truth about the Holy Spirit*, as the soul of the Church" (DV 26). Briefly, the missiological development promoted by Vatican II is rooted in the Spirit's action, manifested within the Council itself (RM 1-2).

More specifically, the Council enabled the Church to be open to the modern world, to seek new approaches and new forms of evangelization, to discern the Spirit's presence within secular movements and events. Dialogue with the world is no longer something just useful for the Church; it is necessary because the Spirit also speaks through the world. Secular reality manifests humanity's legitimate desires and aspirations, mankind's struggle for justice and human dignity; thus, mission demands that Christians see that the Spirit of God is present within these developments (*"Spiritus Dei... huic evolutioni adest"* – GS 26). Or again, the Spirit "is not only *close to this world* but *present* in it, and in a sense *immanent*, penetrating it and giving it life from within" (DV 54). Mission requires an in-depth discernment of all the social, political, economic, cultural and religious signs of the times in today's world (GS 4; RM 28-29, 32).

This vision of the Spirit's presence within the world is foundational to the development of an inductive method of theologizing or of doing critical pastoral-theological reflection. This method takes for granted that its subject matter is the *"humanum"* (humanity, human history and society, human progress, human dignity, the human family). Immediately, the oft-quoted principle of John Paul II springs to mind: "man is the primary route that the Church must travel in fulfilling her mission: *he is the primary way for the church...* a way that, in a sense, is the basis of all the other ways that the Church must walk" (RH 14; also: SD p. 5; DV 58, 67).

Approaching theology in this fashion means beginning with "what is going on in human society and the world," with local cultural realities and values, with the traditions and aspirations of people. In short, the world and human reality "set the agenda" for this approach; yet tradition, scripture, the magisterium and social teaching are not excluded; they are essential to the method because they inform the pastoral-theological reflection process.

Mission today takes note of this inductive theological and pastoral method, because through it *local theologies evolve* under the Spirit's guidance. These theologies (pneumatology itself!) develop from below as Christians prayerfully reflect in the light of revelation on events, movements, and realities of the local Church. In this manner, the entire Church is enriched with vibrant theologies as she listens to what the Spirit is saying to the Churches (Rev. 2:7, 11, 17, 29; 3:6, 13, 22).

An appreciation of the Spirit focuses the missioner upon the Spirit's activity both in and beyond the Christian community. Every dimension of mission must follow the Spirit's lead and promptings (RM 28-30).

Within the Christian community, the Spirit is known as a personal presence, as Person-love, as Person-gift (DV 10, 22, 50). The Spirit is a personal companion to the missioner, giving the grace of a mission vocation and enabling one to discern and be capable of fulfilling the mission entrusted to every evangelizer. The fruits of the Spirit (Gal. 5:22-23) – love, joy, peace, patience, kindness, goodness, faithfulness, gentleness and self-control – are the constant guides given the evangelizer for discerning authentic missionary activity.

The Holy Spirit, sent by Christ, keeps missioners faithful to the life, teachings, and mission of Jesus himself. The Spirit is Counsellor, Intercessor, Advocate, and Comforter; the Spirit's fourfold functions are teaching, accusing, comforting and consoling. In a word, the missioner would be paralyzed without the manifold and abiding presence of the Spirit.

The entire Church is richly endowed by the Spirit with a variety of spiritual gifts (I Cor. 12:4-11). Each gift has a special function and enables Christians to mature together into a united, yet diverse, community. This fundamentally charismatic structure of the Church is, in itself, a special gift. An evangelization process worthy of the name can best be promoted by evoking all the treasures of the Christian charismatic community (RM 61-76). Only in this manner can a Church, enriched with diverse gifts, hope to bear fruit in mission; varied charisms are given to meet all the unique demands made upon a Church-in-mission.

An enthusiastic enumeration of the charisms found within the Church must not lead to the supposition of a monopoly of the Spirit by the Christian community. From the time of Vatican II (GS 38), there have been repeated admonitions for Christians to keep their horizons open to the Spirit's activity in the world. The bishops' declaration from the 1974 Synod on Evangelization affirmed "the Holy Spirit's action, which overflows the bounds of the Christian community" (EMW 11). One can often see the "effects of the Spirit of truth operating outside the visible confines of the Mystical Body" (RH 6). In his encyclical "On the Holy Spirit in the Life of the Church and the World," Pope John Paul II reiterated that the Second Vatican Council "reminds us of the Holy Spirit's activity also 'outside the visible body of the Church'" (DV 53). And, most recently, the same Pope noted that the "Spirit's presence and activity affect not only individuals but also society and history, peoples, cultures and religions" (RM 28).

Acceptance of the activity of the Spirit, "who distributes His charismatic gifts as He wills for the common good" (AG 23), has clear ramifications for inculturation as well as for an approach to non-Christian religions.

In inculturating her program of evangelization, the Church must "share in cultural and social life..., be familiar with national and religious traditions, gladly and reverently laying bare the seeds of the Word that lie hidden in them..., [and] illumine these treasures with the light of the gospel" (AG 11). The Church "must be acquainted with culture..., heal and preserve it..., permeate and transform it" (AG 21). Enlightened by the Spirit, evangelizers accept that "Christian life can be accommodated to the genius and the dispositions of each culture" (AG 22); additional references are: AG 4; LG 17; GS 26, 38, 44. Missioners today are asked to accept this understanding of mission as the Spirit's lead in fostering the attitudes and approaches fundamental to the inculturation of the Gospel. Yes, all mission is *"a sending forth in the Spirit"* (RM 22).

The Church's openness to the followers of the great religious traditions/faiths draws guidance from discerning the Spirit "who blows where he wills." The Church "rejects nothing that is true and holy in these religions. She looks with sincere respect upon those ways of conduct and life... [because they] often reflect a ray of that truth which enlightens all men... [She acts] prudently and lovingly, through dialogue and collaboration with the followers of other religions... [to]

acknowledge, preserve, and promote the spiritual and moral goods found among these men" (NA 2). This insight, acceptance, and active collaboration with other religious traditions (especially in Asia) repeatedly manifest the Spirit's abundant inspiration (cf. RM 55-57).

Note also the interrelationship between efforts toward inculturation and dialogical interaction with other religions, cultures, and world views. Only when the Church is enriched through interfaith dialogue does she have the sensitivity and awareness to truly inculturate/contextualize the Christian message. Missioners readily affirm the Spirit's role in guiding the Church toward a more authentic inculturation as she travels the path of interreligious dialogue (cf. RM 52-54).

In interfaith dialogue, as well as in the inculturation process, the missionary, theologian, or Christian community and the Spirit act as partners. There is always collaboration among these agents; the Holy Spirit is the internal agent, guiding the efforts of the external agents of evangelization. The techniques and human efforts toward inculturation and dialogue are fruitful due to the discreet action of the Spirit; also, it is the Spirit alone (EN 75) who changes people's hearts, minds, and attitudes *(metanoia)* so that true inculturation and open dialogue can succeed.

In this entire process, the evangelizer comes to realize that the Spirit has actually preceded all human efforts. Yes, it is clear that "He visibly anticipates the apostles' action, just as He unceasingly accompanies and directs it in different ways" (AG 4). The Spirit's presence has constantly been at work in the world – even before Christ was glorified (AG 4; DV 25), even back to the beginning of creation (DV 53).

The "world-wide" action of the Spirit accomplishes another marvel: "The Holy Spirit gives to everyone the possibility of coming into contact with the paschal mystery in the way that God alone knows" (GS 22). This affirmation of Vatican II is recalled by John Paul II in his encyclical on the Holy Spirit (DV 53), and he also uses the same passage to elucidate the meaning of the October 27, 1986, Assisi Day of Prayer, which brought together representatives of many of the world's religious groups (ADP 4). This unique statement is quoted verbatim three times in the recent mission encyclical (RM 6, 10, 28); it obviously is a central theme in the missionary outlook of Pope John Paul II. The Church enthusiastically continues her mission of promoting such new manifestations of the Spirit's unifying action in the world.

The involvement of Christians in promoting Kingdom-building movements in the world emerges from her trust that God's Spirit "with a marvelous providence directs the unfolding of time and renews the face of the earth" (GS 26; RM 28). This vision enables evangelizers to see the hand of God in today's social-political movements as they struggle for freedom, justice, love and peace. Such efforts in the secular arena are an invitation to the Church to adopt new ways of mission, to encourage personal and social liberation, and to be more innovative in her forms of witness, service and dialogue. The Reign of God is readily promoted as the Church collaborates with (but does not dominate) these developments.

Finally, two additional themes are noted because they show the mutual links between pneumatology and missiology. The inspiring emergence of laity-in-mission is a sign of renewal; Vatican II has encouraged the Church to appreciate "the unmistakable work of the Holy Spirit in making the laity today even more conscious of their own responsibility and inspiring them everywhere to serve Christ and the Church" (AA 1; RM 71-72). In addition, the ecumenical dimension evident in approaches to evangelization today is best contextualized by witnessing the Spirit's movement within all Christian ecclesial communities. The Catholic Church recognizes that the Christian Churches "are joined with us in the Holy Spirit" (LG 15) and that "the Spirit of Christ has not refrained from using them as means of salvation" (UR 3). Ecumenical cooperation in mission is founded upon faith in the Spirit's capacity to use the diversity of the many Christian ecclesial communities to advance Kingdom and Gospel values in human society.

Pneumatology and missiology have witnessed a mutual renewal in the twenty-five years since Vatican II. This growth has challenged the Church and, in particular, it has enabled her to probe the foundations of mission. Evangelizers themselves have come to trustingly discern and follow the Spirit's promptings; they now recognize more clearly that (as the sequence of Pentecost says): *sine tuo numine nihil est in homine,* that without the Spirit's enlightenment nothing is within humanity, nothing is humanly possible. Mission theology, approaches, and techniques can never dispense with or underestimate the action of the befriending Spirit (GS 3; EN 75; RM 21-30).

For the Church to be vibrant and alive in mission, she must repeatedly be renewed and transformed by the Spirit. Her prayer unceasingly invokes the empowering Spirit:

Glory to you, Holy Spirit!
>You brooded over chaos...
>You inspired prophets and evangelists...
>You liberated the early Church for mission...
And still you brood over,
>inspire and liberate us,
We praise you!

In simplicity and profundity, the Church and her evangelizers pray with constantly renewed vigor: Come, Holy Spirit!

Led by the Spirit into the Paschal Mystery

Mission and Dialogue have occupied center stage in Catholic circles in recent years; there is a renewal of evangelical consciousness in the church. Mission, which for decades had been a poor stepchild, is again recognized as central to the community of Jesus' disciples.

Two mission resources have helped focus this renewed interest in evangelization. They are the mission encyclical *Redemptoris Missio* (RM) and the document *Dialogue and Proclamation* (D&P); both were released in early 1991. The encyclical presents a comprehensive vision of Catholic mission thought and practice; the second document deals specifically with the role of interfaith dialogue within the church's mission of evangelization.

This brief piece seeks to highlight a particular theme of the documents mentioned; in fact, it will focus on a unique quote. One reads that, as Christian believers, *"we must hold that the Holy Spirit offers to all the possibility of being made partners, in a way known to God, in the Paschal mystery."*

This is the only statement that is cited more than once in the entire mission encyclical (RM 6, 10, 28). Its origin is the Vatican II document on the Church in the Modern World (GS 22). Pope John Paul II has referred to it repeatedly (RH 8, 13, 18; DV 53; ADP 4; CA 47). Two key documents from the Pontifical Council for Interreligious Dialogue cite it consistently (D&M 24, 37; D&P 15, 28, 68). Asian as well as Latin

American Bishops Conferences use it in their documents (FABC I, 28; FABC V, 1.4, 6.4; FABC-OE, 49; CELAM Puebla 1117).

Given the panorama and frequency with which this Vatican II passage is currently employed, one can validly assert that it expresses an important missiological insight. It is probably one of the guiding theological principles of John Paul II's vision of mission with the followers of the world's living faiths. It bears a close exegesis for its usefulness within contemporary mission theory (orthodoxy) and practice (orthopraxis).

ROLE OF THE HOLY SPIRIT

No mission theology today is complete without an adequate understanding of pneumatology (Theology of the Holy Spirit). The Spirit is present and active – both in and beyond the churches (RH 6). Missionaries continually recognize in peoples, cultures, and traditions many wholesome effects caused by the grace and charity of the Holy Spirit (RM 28-29). God's loving design of salvation is certainly inclusive of these positive manifestations of the Spirit's gifts.

One must also note that the Holy Spirit is not some unknown impersonal force. The Spirit of God is also the Spirit of Jesus Christ crucified and risen, a fact that must not be overlooked in examining the particular way in which the Spirit is active in the world, in people's lives.

In the Christian mystery two perspectives – the Christological and the Pneumatological – are concomitantly present; it would be erroneous to set them in opposition. As the Christian accompanies the believers of other faiths in a dialogue of life, one discovers and discerns the active presence and life-giving influence of Jesus' Holy Spirit. In technical missiological terms, Christians always operate from the perspective of a "Pneumatological Christocentrism."

THE SPIRIT'S UNIVERSAL ACTIVITY

The brief text under consideration notes that "the Holy Spirit offers to *all*" his grace-filled gifts. They reach all persons, all peoples, all socio-cultural situations and every aspect of human life (RM 10). Mission must never confine its search for the promptings of Jesus' Spirit to any narrow, "churched" reality or circumstances; mission is inherently universal – or it is not mission at all (Heb. 2:9).

Underlying the Spirit's universal activity is a profound anthropological truth: the fundamental unity of all humanity. The entire human family and all its members have the same divine origin, reflected in the divine image they all bear. God's loving design of salvation is one and universal – including every human being who comes into the world (I Tim. 2:4). The Holy Spirit, "who is mysteriously present in the heart of every person" (ADP 11), does not operate in a selective, niggardly manner; the Spirit offers "to *all*" his gracious gifts (RM 29).

It is within this general framework of our radical human unity as well as the universality of God's design that Christians must appreciate other religions and the authentic values they contain. The ultimate vocation of all humanity is in fact one and divine; integral evangelization never loses sight of God's universal plan and the Spirit's universal presence and activity.

SHARING THE PASCHAL MYSTERY

At the heart of Christ's redemptive action within the loving design of the Father stands the Paschal event. Church documents as well as contemporary theologians employ the term "paschal mystery" to capsulize the total Easter mystery of Jesus' passion, resurrection, ascension, and sending of the Spirit at Pentecost. All of Christian life is considered to be paschal; Christians continually share Christ's dying and rising in their daily lives; the Eucharist is their paschal meal.

In this context, the word "mystery" is to be taken in its technical theological and biblical sense: the *"mysterion"* focuses on God's loving plan of salvation for all peoples; it is centered in Christ and reflects the wisdom of God; through it the meaning of the whole of human history is manifested; its pattern is always "paschal," moving through death to renewed life.

Life itself has a paschal configuration; all people struggle to move from darkness to light, from captivity to freedom, from dryness to growth, from alienation to union. Or again, life has an internal dynamic focused on the movement from death to life in all of its dimensions: from falsehood to truth, from apathy to responsibility, from margination to participation, from loneliness and isolation to universal communion, from sin to grace.

Life's paschal paradigm (universally shared by all peoples – whatever terminology may be used) offers a most productive entrée for followers of all faiths to enter into dialogue. It builds upon our common humanity and experience. This paradigm is pregnant with possibilities to respond to profound human needs and to forge authentic bonds of solidarity and mutual compassionate respect.

The paschal nature of all life and experience continually provides openings for a deep human-divine encounter. It allows the human-divine life experience of one person (Christian, Buddhist?) to encounter the human-divine life experience of another individual (Muslim, Hindu?). Herein lies a rich potential to plumb the depths of authentic interpersonal and interfaith dialogue.

This heart-to-heart encounter is a direct effect of the Holy Spirit's action in bringing peoples into a sharing of the paschal mystery. The Spirit continually penetrates the concrete lives and histories of people from within and offers them a real mutual participation in the paschal mystery. Yes, for the Christian it will certainly be explicitly Christological. However, the identical experience, although often in an incoate form, is continually lived by all peoples – whatever their particular religious affiliation.

Unfortunately and even scandalously, the examples of the lived paschal mystery and the "passion of humanity" abound in the world today: war, famine, oppression, poverty, sickness, hatred, death; human suffering is massive – even pandemic. This suffering must never be depersonalized; it always has human faces! And, it is precisely in these contexts where God seems absent or hidden *(deus absconditus)* that a missiology of *theologia crucis* is eminently realistic; mission and dialogue are always cruciform.

It is in situations of apparent God-foresakenness that the explicitly Christian Paschal Mystery is intimately and validly linked with the paschal mystery of all humanity. The world knows only too well the ongoing passion of humankind, the suffering of "crucified peoples" in all times and places. The paschal paradigm has the power to illumine the truth of the suffering that is omnipresent in creation and history as well as the truth of God in relation to suffering. This is not to suggest that there are easy solutions or to minimize the harsh reality of suffering. The passion of humanity continually presents believers of all faiths a *kairos* moment for authentic dialogue and human solidarity.

WAYS KNOWN BY GOD

An important truth about mission is asserted when it is understood as belonging to God; it is "God's project." This frees Christians from believing that through some power of their own mission progresses or bears fruit. The principal agent of mission is always the Holy Spirit (RM 21, 30).

When the paschal paradigm of all people's experience fruitfully encounters the Christic form of paschality, it is precisely due to the action of the Spirit. It is the Holy Spirit's mission to effect within Christians (and to provide the possibility to all others) the redemption accomplished for all on the single occasion of Christ's Paschal Mystery. In other words, it is the Holy Spirit who communicates personally a sharing in that objective redemption of Christ's Paschal Mystery.

When the Church explicitly states that this salvific gift ("the Paschal Mystery") is universally available ("offers to all"), it clearly affirms God's design for everyone's salvation. This is effected by God's action alone ("Holy Spirit").

At the same time that the Church vigorously asserts the reality of the gift, it notes that other ways by which one shares the Paschal Mystery are "known to God." In short, God's ways far exceed our human grasp; yet, we have every reason to trust God's boundless generosity which provides all people – "without any exception" (RH 14) – the possibility of incorporation into the Paschal Mystery.

These assertions only serve to strengthen the fact that mission remains "God's project." We cannot bring about the paschal mystery for ourselves; as the salvific mystery of death and resurrection, by its very nature it can only be received. When, how, who, what manner – all are questions entrusted to God's patience and love.

IMPLICATIONS FOR MISSION

The foregoing brief commentary on a popular yet profound quote used in contemporary Catholic missiology has opened a world of creative insights into mission theology and practice. The insights it affirms are many: (1) the active role of the Spirit in all missionary activity; (2) the universality of proffered grace and salvation; (3) the common paschal experience (dying-rising) of all humanity as an avenue linking all peoples of faith; (4) sharing the paschal mystery as an *experiential* basis for interreligious dialogue and human solidarity; (5) mission conceived within a theology of "Pneumatological-Christocentrism"; (6) mission as "God's project"; (7) a clear linkage of orthodoxy with orthopraxis; (8) the need for missioners to appreciate God's love and patience, to take their mission approaches from the very heart of the Gospel's paschal message, and to align themselves with God's suffering involvement with all humanity.

Any insightful reader will quickly note that this presentation leaves many rich ideas underdeveloped; further depth and nuance would demand a greatly expanded treatment. Yet, clear signposts have been indicated for fruitful approaches to mission and interreligious dialogue based in pneumatology and paschality. Evangelizers and missioners are personally invited to re-image their lives so they may become truly "paschal missionaries."

Life and Mission Today

7

Sketching Mission in Asia

Asia's faces are countless; they are changing and challenging; they are both ancient and modern; they invite and baffle simultaneously. As home to over 60% of humanity, Asia is vast and richly diverse. China, the world's largest nation, contains nearly one-fourth of the globe's population. What author would dare make general statements about this multifaceted continent?

Asia, the territory of the great religious traditions of Buddhism, Hinduism, Confucianism, and Taoism, is also home to the world's two largest Islamic countries: Indonesia and Bangladesh. Christians of all denominations represent about two percent of the burgeoning Asian masses; and, of these Christians, more than one-half live in one country alone, the Philippines.

With the exception of a few affluent countries like Japan, Taiwan, South Korea, and Singapore, the Asian continent is largely poor. Poor – not in human qualities, values, insights and potential – but poor in that they are deprived of access to material development. Many peoples live under social, economic and political realities which are unjust and oppressive. They search for liberation and freedom – often by difficult paths and with mixed success.

To be in mission in Asia of the 1990s demands a perceptive analysis of diverse situations from Hong Kong to Ho Chi Minh City, from Taiwan to Thailand, from Pakistan to Papua New Guinea. Knowing the context, perceiving current trends and social movements, discerning the signs: all these are essential tasks in living and preaching the Good News of Jesus. And, all would certainly be impossible without firm faith and a deep trust in the presence of the guiding Spirit.

To capture and focus Asian realities – with their concomitant challenges – diverse approaches or analytical thematizations may prove helpful. This brief piece proposes to present three such capsulizations: (a) the "three Cs" of crown, culture and cross; (b) the integral nature of evangelization; and, (c) Asian local Churches in dialogue. Each speaks to the task of mission in contemporary Asia.

MISSION REALITIES

The "three Cs" are merely a catchy handle to describe the changes and transformation within Asia since the Second World War. Succinctly expressed, major shifts have taken place in political and economic life (crown), in social and cultural realities (culture), in religious and church life (cross). These evolutions (and sometimes revolutions) have momentous implications – requiring perceptive analysis by local Churches and missioners alike.

The crown, the ruling power, has changed in many Asian countries – beginning in 1945 (Indonesia), in 1946 (Philippines), in 1947 (India) and continuing across the continent. The yoke of colonialism has been rejected and neo-colonialism is resisted. One sees newly independent and developing nations. This is a key "sign of the times" – as John XXIII so clearly noted in his 1963 encyclical *Pacem in Terris* (Peace on Earth).

The understanding of "culture" has grown and matured; in fact, an authentic view has now emerged. Unfortunately, many Church-people had been subservient to European-Western culture as the norm of all societies; it had dominated local cultures, languages, symbols and expression. This view of a "normative culture" has been dismissed; all cultures are equally valid. The diversity of culture and social organization is but an expression of the diversity of humanity. In short, people live their authentic human identity in diversified expression. No culture may be judged to be "inferior" or another be said to be "superior"!

The "third C" refers to the sphere of religion; mission was exclusively identified with conversion to Christianity, to the cross. Frequently, this view saw European Christendom as the paradigm of accepting the faith. The socio-cultural expression often obscured the core of Jesus' message. To accept Christianity meant accepting Christendom as a "package-deal" with all its Western trappings. Today the Church admits her past limitations and seeks to be in mission in more authentic ways.

Any facile expression of a complex phenomenon like evangelization will have its limitations; this is true of the expression of mission realities in the "three Cs." Yet, it may assist one in appreciating the vast changes that have occurred in mission in recent decades. We have moved from colonialism to independent nations, from Western "normative" culture to cultural diversity, from one incarnation or expression of the faith to a pluriformity of authentic expressions. Mission views these evolutions with serious attention.

INTEGRAL EVANGELIZATION

The Church has not changed her identity, her teaching, her faithfulness as the community of Jesus' disciples. However, the style and approaches, the emphases and expressions, have definitely been rethought. And, the reformulation has been influenced by a better perception of the politico-economic, socio-cultural, and religious realities of today's changed and changing world. In brief, the *content* of Jesus' message remains perennially valid but the *context* is constantly undergoing transformation (even radical change as the "three Cs" would indicate).

The Second Vatican Council promoted and facilitated this reappraisal; it encouraged the Church to view herself as the Church in/ within the modern world. To preach the gospel and fulfill her mission, she must scrutinize the changing signs of the times and then interpret them with gospel fidelity for every generation and culture (GS 4; RM 28-29, 32). This task demands viewing evangelization in a unified and holistic manner (RM 11, 20, 24-36, 41-60, 83); only with such a vision can the Church promote the integral liberation of peoples.

Current missiological thought in the Church views holistic evangelization as having at least five dimensions or components. Mission demands: witness of Christian living; the service of humanity; interreligious dialogue and inculturation; explicit gospel proclamation; and liturgical-sacramental life. In brief, the totality of Christian mission embraces all these five elements (RM 41). A word about each dimension is needed.

Mission is already present by the witness of Christians in their daily living of the gospel. As they share community with both Christians as well as the followers of other faiths, they give a silent proclamation of the Good News. Their integration of Gospel values with daily life can speak a powerful message. Pope Paul VI called this the "initial act of evangelization" (EN 21; cf. RM 42-43). And yet, Christians remain humble, knowing they "bear this treasure in earthen vessels" (II Cor. 4:7).

Service of humanity, activities for social development, and the struggle against poverty and the structures producing it – all constitute a proclamation particularly relevant in today's world. All strata of society need transformation; gospel values must challenge both individual and social selfishness. Modern society is often more open to hear a message spoken in authentic, simple service rather than in lengthy, windy words!

An integrated view of evangelization appreciates interreligious and intercultural dialogue in which Christians meet the followers of other religious traditions; they join together, walking towards truth and working hand-in-hand in projects of common concern. Such "dialogue" clearly means more than "mere discussion"; it includes all constructive interfaith/intercultural relations directed towards mutual understanding and enrichment. The minority situation of Christianity in Asia demands this approach; frequently it is the most loving, practical, and beneficial response possible by sincere Christians.

In addition, gospel proclamation and catechesis, instruction in scripture and church teaching, liturgical life and prayer-contemplation are also tasks of evangelization. They are requirements for a healthy, vibrant Christian community. Realistically, every faith-community needs its inner life strengthened and nourished as it seeks to be an authentic witness to Jesus' love in today's complex world.

As was emphasized earlier, the totality of Christian mission today embraces all these elements. All are evangelization; all are mission. Witness of life, service of humanity, interreligious/intercultural dialogue are not simply "preparatory phases" to the "real preaching" of the Good News; they must not be termed only "indirect evangelization"; all these are integral elements of the local Church's total mission of evangelization (EN 17, 24; RM 41). They follow the example of Jesus who lived mission within an integrated and multi-faceted vision of God's Kingdom.

APPROACH OF DIALOGUE

In light of vastly changed realities and desiring to implement an integral approach to evangelization, the local Churches of Asia have focused their attention on the approach of dialogical mission. Already during the first plenary assembly of the Federation of Asian Bishops' Conferences (Taipei, 1974), the primary focus of the task of evangelization was identified as "the building up of a truly local Church." And FABC I noted that "this means concretely a Church in continuous, humble and loving dialogue with the living traditions, the cultures, the religions – in brief, with all the life-realities of the people..." (FABC I, 9 & 11).

If Asia is the continent of many peoples, many cultures, and many religions, then all local Churches that are truly rooted and incarnate – truly Asian – will be in dialogue with indigenous peoples, cultures, and religions. In brief, this is the formula for authentic development of the local Church, whether in Taiwan or Hong Kong, Korea or Malaysia. The formula is deceptively simple; the implementation has begun but awaits growth and maturity.

A closer look at this triple, dialogical approach reveals the enormous task facing Asia's Christian communities. They are small in number; compared to national populations, the local Churches are only "little flocks" (e.g. 0.18% in Bangladesh; 0.3% in Japan; 1.5% in Taiwan; 0.41% in Thailand). Yet, they are called to be missionary; the Church exists to evangelize; it is her deepest identity. Mission is not only an "added decoration, a marginal element"; it is "a constitutive dimension of our Catholic faith" as Paul VI has proclaimed.

The "first dialogue" of Asia's local churches is with the masses among whom she lives. Some of the most densely populated nations of the world are found in Asia – with Bangladesh leading the list. This dialogue will directly involve the Church in peoples' movements, promoting programs of conscientization, organization and development.

Based on a faith-vision of human dignity, Christians will foster authentic justice and peace – with a keen eye to non-violent social transformation. Although the Asian local Churches are very small, through this interaction they will not withdraw or develop a "minority complex"; they will be productive actors within the broader society.

The first dialogue propels the local Church towards another interaction – dialogue with culture. She must "inculturate" by sinking deep roots among all peoples whose life and history she gladly makes her own.

Asia's bishops envision a local Church who shares "whatever belongs to that people: its meanings and its values, its aspirations, its thoughts and its language, its songs and its artistry. Even its frailties and failings it assumes, so that they too may be healed." The Church actually seeks the dialogical evangelization of cultures.

People, their culture and religion are intimately intertwined. This fact demands a third interaction: dialogue with the living faith traditions of Asia. Local Churches in Asia have made considerable progress in the theology and practice of interreligious dialogue.

The religions of Asia are accepted as "significant and positive elements in the economy of God's design of salvation." Why? As the Asian Church has stated, they contain "profound spiritual and ethical meanings and values"; they are "the treasury of the religious experience of our ancestors"; they are "the home of their contemplation and prayer"; they are imbedded in "the histories and cultures of our nations" (FABC I, 14).

No evangelization will be lasting and fruitful if it does not travel the path of this three-fold dialogue. In fact, any approach which does not interact deeply with the many peoples, cultures, and religions will remain foreign to Asian soil. It would only be a partial, fragmentary, superficial, and ineffectual vision of the task of mission in contemporary Asia.

CONCLUSION

Three vignettes, three capsulizations, three thumb-nail sketches attempting to describe the complexity of mission in Asia – only this much has been provided in this brief piece. Missioners and local Churches alike recognize the challenges they face. Yet, they are faith-full people, trusting the action of the Spirit to guide them. They continually go forward in this new age of mission in Asia; they are filled with hope. They believe that mission is "God's project" (RM 24) and will happily bear fruit in conformity with the patience of God's loving design for all humanity.

8

Exploring Popular Religiosity for Proclamation

Evangelization, in the experience of missionaries, catechists and liturgists, is immensely enriched by drawing upon the insights and rituals of popular religiosity. In diverse cultural milieus, pastoral agents are discovering that their task of announcing the Gospel is facilitated and enhanced through the creative use of popular ritual and dramatics. In a word, folk religious practices are a resource-for-evangelization awaiting full exploration.

Often culturally unique, local traditions and pageants can creatively portray core themes of Christianity and biblical faith. Such inculturated proclamation originates in the encounter of life and faith; it is then celebrated through the pageantry and festivity of popular religiosity. This approach to liturgy and evangelization enables communities to artistically portray their lived Christian identity.

Lively expressions of a community's faith-life need not raise undue anxieties about dogmatic orthodoxy or faithfulness to biblical texts. On the contrary, popular forms of piety should be welcomed as tools of evangelization, because dramatics, pageantry, socio-religious rituals and festivity can often constitute, in themselves, an actual proclamation of biblical faith!

Pope Paul VI's famous apostolic exhortation on evangelization in the modern world devoted a lengthy section to the role that popular piety should play in announcing the Good News. While noting its possible limitations, the pope optimistically asserted that "if it is well oriented, above all by a pedagogy of evangelization, it is rich in values;... one must be sensitive to it, know how to perceive its interior dimensions and undeniable values.... When it is well oriented, this popular religiosity can be more and more for multitudes of our people a true encounter with God in Jesus Christ" (EN 48).

RESURRECTION RITUALS IN THE FIESTA ISLANDS

The story is told that one Easter St. Peter noticed that many Filipinos were absent from heaven. Upon inquiry, he discovered that they all had returned to earth to celebrate the Resurrection festivities in their own hometowns. This humorous Filipino tale captures the magnetic quality of the Easter ritual, known locally as the "meeting"; it dramatizes the encounter of the risen Christ and his mother on Easter morning.[1]

In the darkness before the crack of dawn, two processions begin wending their way through the streets of the town. Literally, several hundreds join the activities which begin around 4:00 a.m.

One procession is composed of the townsmen. This all-male group follows the statue of the risen Christ, clad in gold-embroidered white silk and holding his victory standard. The statue is borne aloft by young men who consider it a unique privilege to be chosen to carry the risen Jesus.

Another procession, composed of the women of the town, follows the statue of the sorrowful mother *(mater dolorosa)*. She is in mourning, her face covered by a black veil; her hands are clasped in sorrow. The somber mood of Good Friday dominates the two processions.

Both groups, praying and singing as they follow their separate routes, emerge into the town square where additional crowds are waiting. With coordinated movements, they simultaneously approach the arch of "meeting." The first light of dawn is breaking; the little male and female angels are positioned around the arch; flowers and decorations abound.

A white-clad angel is lowered ever so carefully from the pulleys inside the arch. She intones the *Regina Caeli Laetare, Alleulia*; then, to the accompaniment of the band, all the choirs of angels on the arch break into their Easter chants. At the end of their singing, the lead angel slips her finger through a ring atop the Virgin Mother's black veil. As the angel is slowly raised up on the arch, she removes the veil and reveals the gleaming ivory face of the Virgin. Mary meets her risen Son – to the wild, yet prayerful, enthusiasm of the expectant crowd. The band strikes up a rousing anthem and the faithful enter the church to continue celebrating in Word and Sacrament the Easter liturgy. Christ is truly risen!

DRAMATIZED – YET AUTHENTIC – FAITH AND PROCLAMATION

The foregoing scene of resurrection encounter – meeting the risen Jesus – is true proclamation in pageantry, drama, and song. It is eminently faithful to the Gospel narratives of the resurrection, which themselves can be understood as "faith dramas."

A survey of the appearances of the risen Jesus reveals a rich variety in the different scriptural accounts by the evangelists; they were addressing different communities with unique theological interests and purposes. Despite great divergence in the details, each author seeks to communicate the same fundamental experience: the crucified one is risen and alive! Surely, this was also the Virgin Mary's experience.[2]

New Testament exegetes (e.g. Dodd, Lane, Léon-Dufour) detect the presence of a pattern in most resurrection encounters.[3] The Gospels are perceived to include five paradigmatic elements in their narratives:

a. The mood is one of confusion, sadness, fear, disappointment, despondency; Jesus' followers are in darkness and their minds are clouded (Lk. 24:21; Jn. 20:11, 20:19; Mk. 16:3).

b. The initiative for the encounter comes from Jesus; he accompanies the disciples wandering in their confusion (Lk. 24:15; Jn. 20:19, 21:4; Mt. 28:9, 28:18).

c. There is a word of greeting or a gesture of peace (Jn. 20:19, 20:26; Mt. 28:9; Lk. 24:36).

d. The climactic point is reached and centers on the experience of recognition (Jn. 20:16, 20:20, 20:28, 21:7, 21:12; Lk. 24:31; Mt. 28:9, 28:17).

e. A mission command from Jesus concludes the encounter (Mt. 28:18-20, 28:10; Mk. 16:15; Lk. 24:28; Jn. 20:17, 20:21, 21:15 ff.).

A retracing of this biblical-liturgical-catechetical paradigm of the resurrection is now possible in tandem with the dramatic "meeting"/ "encounter" that Filipino popular religiosity celebrates early on Easter morn. In fact, the parallelism is almost self-evident:

a. Darkness reigns as the drama begins to unfold before dawn; it appears that the gloom and hopelessness of death have been victorious. Mary is weeping.

b. Jesus draws near to his friends wandering through the streets of town; the dual processions present Jesus looking for his sorrowful mother.

c. Jesus' word of greeting is placed on the lips of the interpreting angel: "Rejoice, O Queen of Heaven, Alleluia."

d. The climactic moment of recognition is the central focus; Mary's black veil of sadness is removed to reveal her joyful face carved from polished ivory; her facial expression proclaims: "It is the Lord"!

e. The crowds move into the church to hear the scriptures proclaim their mandate to be witnesses of the resurrection; the sacrament of the Eucharist empowers the faithful for their mission.

Reflection further reveals that the biblical pattern of resurrection encounter, so poignantly dramatized in the inculturated Easter pageantry found throughout the Philippines, is a catechetical paradigm of our own Christian experience. We so often walk in darkness, failing to recognize the reality of Christ among us; he calls us by name to acknowledge his living presence; we need Word and Sacrament to heal our blindness; when we recognize that he lives, we are impelled into mission to announce the Good News to all creation.

IMPETUS FOR INCULTURATED EVANGELIZATION

Commenting on the religious dramatization that surrounds Easter in the Philippines, a Filipino author has correctly noted that the Easter Encounter is "the very crown of the Filipino's *Semana Santa* [Holy Week]."[4] This is a compliment to ordinary people's valid intuitions and insight into scriptural faith; for them, as for St. Paul, meeting and recognizing the risen Lord is central: "If Christ has not been raised, then our preaching is useless and your believing it is also in vain" (I Cor. 15:14).

Taking their cue from each local Church's genius (the Philippine expression is only one example), catechists, evangelizers, and theologians must continue searching for more effective tools of exegesis and inculturated proclamation to announce Christ's living presence. Creative cultural expression ought to address the need of every generation to be "re-evangelized" in its attitudes, motivations, and values. Indigenous proclamation seeks to overcome the split between faith and culture that challenges all societies – be they in first, second, or third world countries.

In a word, then, renewed examination of the role of dramatics, art, song, dance, pageantry, and festivity can certainly be a unique key to making the faith truly alive in people's hearts, imaginations, and daily experiences. These tools can rescue proclamation from the heavily verbal mode (which often dominates in parish catechesis and liturgy). Such creative evangelization effectively reaches a wide audience of diverse ages and backgrounds.

On Easter Sunday ask any Filipino – even a four-year-old child – and you will hear: "Jesus is alive! I saw him meet his mother; Mary is happy and smiling"! Without doubt, here is living liturgy and proclamation! Here is inculturation!

NOTES

1. This ritual is popular throughout the entire country; each region and ethnolinguistic group has its own terminology to describe the event: *salubong* (Tagalog), *pagsugat* (Cebuano), *sabet* (Ilocano), *tonton* (Bicolano), and *abet-abet* (Pangasinan).

2. Peter-Hans Kolvenbach, S.J., "The Easter Experience of Our Lady," *Centrum Ignatianum Spiritualitatis* 19, nos. 2-3 [58-59] (1988) 145-63. See also: Daughters of St. Paul, eds., "Easter Mediation," *The Vatican II Weekday Missal* (Boston: St. Paul Editions, 1975) 717.

3. C.H. Dodd, "The Appearances of the Risen Christ: A Study in Form-Criticism of the Gospels," *More New Testament Studies* (Manchester: M.U.P., 1968) 104-7; Dermot Lane, *The Reality of Jesus* (Dublin, Veritas Publications, 1975) 51-52; X. Léon-Dufour, *Résurrection de Jésus et Message Pascal* (Paris: Éditions du Seuil, 1971) 126-130.

4. Nicanor G. Tiongson, "The Easter Salubong," in Alfredo Roces, ed., *Filipino Heritage* – VII (Manila: Lahing Pilipino Publishing, 1978) 1848.

Enhancing Mission through Reflection

Field missioners and academic missiologists alike both recognize a wide variety of sources or starting-points for constructing contemporary mission theology. Frequently, these approaches are characterized as "from below" (an inductive process) or "from above" (a deductive method). Each has its contribution to make; each has its validity and usefulness. This present piece firmly proceeds along the path of an inductive construction of a vision of mission arising from the lived experience of grassroots missioners.

These distilled reflections on mission in the 1990s for the Asia-Pacific Area are the result of a two-year process of monthly small group pastoral-theological reflection sessions. The "actors" in this ongoing reflection are the 200 Maryknoll missioners living and working on the Asian scene.

As a result of the Ninth General Chapter of the Maryknoll Mission Society held in 1990, an impetus was given to implement a Society-wide reflection process. This was to begin at the base level and later move toward both a regional and area synthesis. The process was not necessarily meant to be exhaustive; it intended to foster a serious reflection on some of the ways overseas missioners might respond to Christ's mission today.

This endeavor to theologize on mission experience comes to flower at an auspicious moment for the Maryknoll Mission Society. Currently,

Maryknoll marks its diamond jubilee of mission work in Asia (1918-1993), having sent its first four missioners to China in the Fall of 1918. Thus, the Asia-Pacific Area has been home for Maryknollers for 75 years; this heritage provides the context for discerning the call to mission in the 1990s – and beyond.

MISSION CONTEXT

Like all missioners worldwide, Maryknollers consider it a privilege to live among a variety of peoples. They note that:

> As foreign missioners we stand in awe at the magnificent cultures and religions in Asia as we encounter their wisdom developed over thousands of years of philosophical, religious, artistic and scientific achievements. We are often astonished at the dynamism of the people, their numbers (60% of the world's population) and youthfulness (50% below 20 years of age). We are constantly discovering the face of God in these people, which makes it all the more painful to see masses of these people crushed by poverty, exploitation, illiteracy, dehumanized living situations, polluted environments, and strife in the name of religion, culture, language or race. We feel these sufferings as sufferings of our own brothers and sisters in Jesus.... Faced with this immense reality we are humbled by the call to be missioners to these people. We realize it is only by the power of God that we can be the Jesus who witnesses to the love of God for these people, the Jesus who heals, who listens, who is sensitive to the differences in persons we encounter, the Jesus who proclaims the Gospel and spends time in prayer with others.

These Asian missioners affirm their dedication to show the "various faces of Jesus to the people they encounter daily." Continuing, they say: "We thank the many people of Asia who have shown the face of Jesus to us." They express the hope that by sharing their experiences in mission others will gain "insight into the hearts of the Maryknoll missioners in Asia-Pacific." They desire that these reflections will "prove helpful in our discerning of the directions in which the Spirit of Jesus wishes to lead us."

EXPERIENCING MISSION

Maryknoll missioners in the Asia-Pacific Area do not presume to speak for other missioners or for the local Church in the countries where they serve. However, they actively seek, based on their mission experience, to discern the presence of the Holy Spirit and the Spirit-indicated directions for effective mission in Asia. These missioners try to pay particular attention to those elements that are future-oriented and provide new insights for mission into the 21st Century.

What follows next is a brief ten-country panoramic presentation of mission contexts and challenges where Maryknollers serve in the Asia-Pacific Area. This is not presented from an idealized mission vision; it is expressed experientially. Yes, it is one perspective; it may be selective; it may lack total comprehensiveness. Yet, it reflects Maryknollers' lived experience; the missioners present it under the heading: *"How We See Mission Being Experienced at the Grassroots."*

BANGLADESH.   Missioners living in Bangladesh are daily confronted with the realities of poverty, more accentuated here than in other countries. They accompany a Church in need of continued re-evangelization. The reality is that the Catholics in Bangladesh are usually financially better off than the average Bangladeshi citizen. All witness a "deculturation" process in which traditional values are being lost because of Western influence and the media.

The missioners have taken a strong option for the poor, but feel a tension that they are not poor like most Bangladeshis. They have a vision of the Church as a community of compassion and seek solidarity with people, walking with them in their daily concerns. Having this vision, they also experience a tension between choosing to work directly with the local Church to assist it develop into a more missionary-oriented, Vatican II-oriented Church or to choose to work directly with the vast population which is both Muslim or Hindu.

Missioners have a clear commitment to developing a contextualized vision of mission. Faith and spirituality is emphasized. While their apostolates have a strong presence and witness element, the missioners constantly examine the quality of their own presence and witness. They feel a need for personal conversion so their lives will be an authentic example of Christian living.

Missioners speaking from their Bangladesh experience are very conscious that they are living interfaith dialogue. For them everything becomes dialogue. They see their daily accompaniment with all Bangladeshis as a form of mission and dialogue. They seek ways to promote unity and harmony within Bangladesh society.

The missioners admit having a strong sense of concern and solidarity for their companion missionaries. This is evidenced by their commitment to overcome great obstacles to gather monthly for prayer, reflection, and mutual support. Their sharing is frequently on a very deep and personal level.

Reaching beyond national boundaries, the Maryknollers working in the Bangladesh Unit strive to foster exchanges between their local Unit and the wider Maryknoll world. They have successfully invited qualified Maryknollers and other missionaries to come for several months to teach in the National Major Seminary or to give other specialized programs for the enrichment of the people and the local Church.

CAMBODIA.   The context of mission in Cambodia is one of conflict, often making it a challenge to sustain hope or faith in the future of Cambodia itself. However, the missioners look for hope and faith to God and God's life in the people. The missioners' experience of Church is very broad: they encounter the Khmers in meetings and worship; they meet the Vietnamese in catechesis and liturgy; they share with the Catholic NGO (Non-Governmental Organizations) community through meetings and reflections; they labor with the local Church in meetings and shared insights on evangelization. These encounters sometimes evoke conflicting emotions and feelings among the missioners themselves.

As evangelizers they preach the Gospel by witnessing to the values of their Christian faith among the Buddhist Khmers; they witness by their deeds to their life of faith and unity with Jesus. They seek to face the effects of colonialism by Thailand, Vietnam, France, and now by the economic powers of the new world order. They recognize the Church's limitations in past eras to adequately value the indigenous and/or world religions in the area. They feel called to repent of the many times they have expected others to use their western language; they combat the pervasive influence that "West is best." They desire to manifest their respect for the indigenous people, seeking to learn from them by using local languages, local terms of reference, local values, outlooks and world views.

The encounter of the missionaries in Cambodia with Buddhism as incarnated in the Khmer people has allowed them to marvel at its capacity for inclusivity. Tolerance, non-judgmental attitudes, and a welcoming stance all flow from Buddhism.

The missioners themselves function as an integrated ecclesial response to mission and have a commitment both to private spiritual reflection and to communal sharing of their spiritual gifts.

The missioners view themselves as committed to a missionary thrust characterized by dialogue and the exchange of ideas, as well as to the spread of Gospel values through lives of love and service, dialogue and encounter. They assume a listening stance and recognize the sacredness of the individual and his/her conscience. As foreign missioners, they believe they can give witness to the universality of the Church and Gospel values. They hope to manifest new vibrant models of Church to some who hold isolationist views of Church. It is in the everyday encounters with others and in the sharing of their lives and beliefs with the people they encounter that these missioners mutually experience dialogue. Mission is founded on mutual respect and the possibility of mutual conversion and a deepening experience of God.

HAWAII. The context of mission in Hawaii is a secularized, "first-world" environment with many unchurched peoples. The islands have experienced a large influx of people from diverse cultures: Filipinos, Chinese, Koreans, Vietnamese, Laotians, Cambodians, Samoans and some Latin Americans. In Hawaii there is also a growing consciousness of indigenous identity as evidenced in the sovereignty movement of the native Hawaiian people.

Founded on their desire for appropriate structures for accomplishing mission and faced with the challenge of decreasing numbers, Hawaiian Maryknollers have engaged themselves in a process of discernment. The result has been a decision to change and simplify their governing structure.

Despite the small number of Maryknollers now serving in the Hawaiian Islands, there is a varied range of apostolates. Some are involved in building up basic Christian communities and promoting lay involvement in ministries. Others are involved in evangelization with the peoples of other faith traditions. Many serve in ministry to the various ethnic groups in addition to the Hawaiian populace: Japanese,

Filipinos, Vietnamese, Cambodians, Chinese, Laotians, Koreans, as well as Spanish-speaking groups and communities.

Realizing the intimate connection between faith and mission, the missioners seek to attend monthly pastoral-theological reflection sessions where they share their spirituality as well as their personal experiences as missioners.

HONG KONG.   The milieu of mission in Hong Kong is currently focused on the changing political reality. There is an urgent need to face the situation of the change of sovereignty in 1997. In the Hong Kong context missioners seek to work in close cooperation with the local Church. Frequently their work becomes pan-Asian, and a number of personnel who are based in Hong Kong fulfill their apostolates in works that reach beyond Hong Kong (e.g. FABC Organizations and Committees).

The missioners have been strengthened in recent years by the growth in numbers of Maryknoll Society members serving in Hong Kong. Some new missioners arrive, and many "veteran" missioners are coming back to Hong Kong after their period of Society service. Locally there is a heavy involvement in social development programs, including prison chaplaincy, a deaf ministry, and housing for the elderly.

There is an upsurge in interest on the part of missioners to serve in new parishes in the geographical location known as the New Territories. They feel some urgency to develop these new areas before 1997 arrives and believe they have gifts to give in this area of parish development.

Missioners in Hong Kong have a keen awareness of the pivotal role that mass communications can play in evangelization throughout Asia. This is evidenced by Maryknollers who are involved in UCAN (Union of Catholic Asian News), the Holy Spirit Study Centre, the *Sunday Examiner*, the Centre for the Progress of Peoples, Social Communications, and graphic arts service.

Looking to develop their personal and spiritual lives as missioners, many come together regularly for pastoral-theological reflection. This promotes an openness to one another and results in a positive influence among all Maryknoll members. Sparked by a Maryknoll-sponsored Area Workshop in Davao City, Philippines, many missioners have shown great interest in and seek healthy ways to reaffirm their role as priest-missioners in the Hong Kong context.

JAPAN. The context of missionary life in Japan is set within an ongoing struggle whereby both Christian and Japanese cultural values are confronted with the challenge to integrate the sacred and the secular. An equilibrium in Japanese society that has prevailed for decades is currently being upset by changed realities. The current situation puts great pressures on family life. There is a large influx of foreign workers, providing new opportunities both for mission in Japanese society as well as for growth in the Church. Missioners struggle to make the Church more responsive to people's situations and problems and to be more missionary itself as a Church.

There is a great desire that the local Church, as well as the missioners themselves, be able to speak to contemporary Japanese society. This is based on a conviction that the Church should have an effect on society at large. However, missionaries are not always sure of the best approaches to speak to Japanese society.

The migrant worker experience is now calling many missioners to a more public and prophetic stance in defense of the human rights of the migrants. Along with the local Church, missioners have a clear commitment to be involved with migrant workers. There is a sense of hope for new opportunities rising from this migrant worker situation. In many local parishes there are English or Spanish Masses; there is an attempt to integrate the foreign workers into the parishes. Local congregations have set up Japanese language programs for the migrant workers. In a spirit of concern and compassion, some parishioners are involved in providing temporary shelter for homeless workers while they search for employment; needed medical attention is often provided for them.

The missioners have a growing appreciation of the value of reflection, of sharing with one another. This is coupled with an awareness and desire for mutual support among the missioners themselves. There is an openness to reconsider mission realities in light of new challenges and to modify mission approaches to address these new situations.

One finds a growing appreciation of the wider dimensions of dialogue in the Japanese context. This has resulted in the discovery that many missioners are actually involved in dialogue activities. Some serve in the dialogue of action and the dialogue of life with Buddhist monks. There is a continued opening to more cooperative efforts with civic groups. Missioners involve themselves in drug and alcohol rehabilitation. All these efforts are seen as falling under the broad umbrella of dialogue. They also offer examples of successful inculturation of international programs based on Christian values (e.g. Alcoholics Anonymous) into the Japanese society and context.

Despite very difficult cultural challenges, the missioners note that they find fulfillment in their work; this is reflected in a spirit of joy and hope in the missioners themselves.

KOREA. The milieu of mission in Korea is a situation in which the Korean people have been divided for almost 50 years. Explorations continue regarding the possibility of promoting eventual unity. Yet, it is a process fraught with tensions and danger. The South has moved from a military dictatorship to a democracy which recently elected its first President with no ties to the military. The new President has taken a strong stand against corruption and military influence. This seems to have calmed student unrest. The economy, which has grown by leaps and bounds, has recently faced stagnation as labor demands a more equitable division of profits. There is currently an influx of foreign workers.

The local Church has a vibrant, active laity. They are strongly involved in all areas of the Church life. The rate of conversions and vocations remains high. The Korean people are comfortable with the piety and practices of traditional elements of the Catholic Church. Most parochial work is now done by diocesan priests.

The Maryknoll Region is currently celebrating 70 years of service in Korea. Missionaries in this context face the task of asking and clarifying their own role in the face of the increasing number of native vocations. Thus, many missioners have moved towards specialized apostolates in service to the local Church. The Maryknoll community in Korea has placed four priests in the Korean-speaking region in northeastern China. In addition, it is the dream of many missioners to eventually have the opportunity to return and work in North Korea. Maryknollers celebrate the fact that they have priests of the Missionary Society of the Philippines working with them in exploring new models of missionary presence.

Foreign missionaries in Korea admit that they have absorbed many traits of the Korean culture in their expression of prayer and spiritual exercises. They note a strong sense of personal and community prayer as well as a respect and love of their missionary priesthood. These are seen as positive resources in expressing their missionary vocation.

NEPAL. The context of mission in Nepal is that of a Hindu kingdom which was only opened to outsiders 40 years ago. It is sandwiched between the two giants of India and China. It is a poor country with very few educated or wealthy people. It is now taking its first faltering steps in democracy. The Nepalese people are bound by the caste system, tribalism, rules and regulations of strict Hinduism and the old bureaucrats. In addition to a dominant Hindu influence, Nepal also has important Buddhist temples.

Conversion to another faith tradition is still forbidden by the Constitution, but since the recent revolution, Christianity can be openly practiced. Currently there is only one Church building in the entire country located in the capital, Kathmandu. There is little or no Church presence elsewhere. Tourism, which is the main industry, has brought several problems of the modern world into this rather medieval society.

The Maryknoll missioners engage in evangelization in Nepal through a variety of works: literacy training, English and vocational courses for adults, assistance for the mentally retarded, programs to meet the needs of 100,000 Bhutanese refugees, as well as the promotion of mutual understanding and acceptance among Muslims, Hindus, and Buddhists. The missioners will soon be involved in a new collaborative project of housing mentally ill women who have been put in jail for lack of other facilities to care for them; a program of rehabilitation is being established.

Maryknollers face a number of problems in this Hindu kingdom: there is the difficulty of obtaining visas; the number of missionaries is small; they face the problem of geographic isolation from one another; they lack a strong, centrally located community which would enable them to have a missionary insertion program for new missioners (currently they are relying on veteran missioners to come to serve in Nepal); they face a unique handicap as foreigners because they are frequently believed to be members of NGOs who bring money, influence, and possible employment.

Missioners in Nepal accept that they have few external aids to be faithful in their religious practices and prayer. A conscious effort must be made to develop one's personal spiritual life. Missioners live daily with the great religions and they are challenged to be open to see God in the people that they meet. When an opportunity is available for them to be together for prayer or Eucharist or socializing, it is a great source of delight for them.

PHILIPPINES. Missioners laboring in the Philippine Islands find themselves working in close cooperation/interaction with the local Church. They serve in an auxiliary role, realizing that "the local Church must increase; we must decrease." Missioners see their role as that of stimulating collaboratively the local Church, bringing new ideas, and exploring apostolates unfamiliar to the local Church. In addition, there continues to be a strong emphasis on preaching and teaching, and the missionaries also actively engage in peace and justice apostolates.

Because the Maryknoll missionary charism is one that transcends provincialism, the missioners seek to be helpful to the local Church as it develops a global vision of mission. One expression of this contribution by the missioners is their deep commitment to promoting the mission response of the local Church. This continues to be accomplished through close cooperation with the Mission Society of the Philippines and the Philippine Catholic Lay Mission Program.

In particular, Maryknollers approach their mission in the context of a deep respect for Philippine values (e.g. hospitality and harmony). The missioners see the possibility of cooperating with other local Churches throughout Asia, especially regarding the question of migrant workers and the missionary response of the Philippine local Church.

Although aware of many new possibilities, the missioners find themselves uncertain at times of how to capitalize on these new opportunities due to the heavy demands of pastoral work and their own declining numbers and energy. The missioners are committed to their own personal and spiritual growth and accomplish this through monthly reflection and prayer groups.

TAIWAN. The context of mission in Taiwan is within a country having an economy which approaches the level of the First World. People are engaged in an intense pursuit of economic progress. Unfortunately, missioners experience that there is little or no interest in Christianity among many people; converts are very few.

The Maryknoll Region in Taiwan has had a constant, strong commitment to the culture and language of the native Taiwanese and aboriginal people. They also have begun new works suited to the needs of the times: a clinical pastoral education project, work with the migrant aborigines, as well as hospitality houses in large cities to reach Catholics who migrate to the city from the countryside.

The missioners are clearly aware that they must go out more among people and not depend on catechists as they have heavily done in the past. They seek to talk to people about Christianity and to have personal contact and communication with them. Mass communications have been stressed: cinema/drama productions, printed material for Sunday Gospel displays, and a variety of newsletters.

As evangelizers, Maryknollers working in Taiwan seek to put emphasis on developing parish communities into missionary communities that are engaged in *ad gentes* mission as well as outreach programs of social concern. For their own personal and faith development, reflection and dialogue are strongly held values by the missionaries. There are monthly reflection groups as well as a specialized contemplative prayer group.

THAILAND. The milieu of mission in Thailand springs from a Unit structure among the missioners. This is an inclusive ecclesial community which operates on a consensus and participation model for all members. Positions of responsibility are open to a variety of members based on their qualifications. Members in the Unit explore various governing structures.

The apostolates of Maryknollers in Thailand are in non-traditional work entered into at the request of the local Church. Such apostolates deal with migrants and tourists in Bangkok and also rural groups in northern Thailand. This brings the missioners into a frequent and direct contact with people of other faith traditions.

The Maryknoll missionary presence of the Thailand Unit is a changing and fluid reality. One-third of the group changes every couple of years; this is due to the presence of many Maryknoll associate personnel. This is both a strength and a weakness for mission. In addition, as is true in many Maryknoll mission areas, there is close cooperation with the Maryknoll Sisters in Thailand.

Missioners in Thailand attempt to integrate their personal life and mission apostolates. They grapple with their own spirituality as they face a new and different culture, a changing Church, and the Buddhist faith tradition. Having been uprooted and having transplanted themselves in a new land, they embrace a spirituality of pilgrimage. They are conscious that they remain part of a sending Church; they also recognize their new connectedness with a variety of people as their brothers and sisters.

In mission these evangelizers explore their personal identity, asking who they are as Christians and as missioners and what God asks of them. This experience, for some a painful one, is that of losing many assumptions based in their culture of origin. This stripping away of assumptions exposes them to the reality of the context of mission in Thailand. They ask who they really are and who God is for them.

The mission apostolates and experience in Thailand reflect a commitment to mission as dialogue. The missioners struggle with a difficult language; they are committed to inculturation. They value their experience as an experimental mission Unit and see this structure as an important model for mission in the 1990s. They assert that it has supported them well in their mission work; it has enabled them to be in collaborative mission, respecting the gifts of diverse vocational charisms.

MISSIONARY VALUES

Based on the foregoing synoptic sketches of mission and in harmony with the inductive reflection process, Maryknollers continually seek to identify important missionary values emerging from the wide diversity of experiences recorded in the 10-country mission panorama. Employing this methodology may be a lengthy – even cumbersome – process; however, it results in a high degree of ownership of mission values, theology, directions and apostolates. This section highlights the *Gospel and missionary values* Asian Maryknollers discern emerging from their mission experience.

Missioners recognize the value of reflection, sharing with one another, mutual support, and shared religious experience through the Eucharist and various prayer forms. Honesty in discussing core issues related to mission is important for group cohesiveness. Issues of spirituality, mission motivation, the struggle to understand culture and to express oneself and communicate the Gospel in this context are a few of the important core issues relating to mission.

Missioners value their sincere attempts to integrate life and mission, to link their identity and their work, to harmonize their spirituality and apostolates.

Dialogue is appreciated both as a missionary attitude and as a form of evangelization. A dialogical attitude includes seeking to understand the religious values of the local people. It incorporates an ongoing search for a deeper experience of culture and religion. It searches for productive ways of cooperating with people of other faiths.

A value for missionaries is to have each local Church more responsive to people's situations, needs and problems. Missioners desire that the local Church itself becomes missionary, whether it is speaking to the local society in an attempt to affect that society at large, or whether it is in moving beyond the borders of the local Church to reach peoples of other lands and cultures.

A high priority for missioners cooperating with local Church and pastoral agents is to be in solidarity with the poor. This involves accompanying them in the suffering arising from violence, exploitation, political and economic domination. It also includes working with the marginated people on the fringes of society. Missioners cast their lot with the local people when they too are faced with experiences of insecurity (e.g. temporary visas, sickness, physical danger, political uncertainties like 1997 in Hong Kong). To recognize this insecurity and to participate in tenuous situations places the missioners in an empathetic solidarity with the poor who constantly have to face life's uncertainties. Missioners can learn from the poor a clear sense of their faith in Jesus and their dependence on God.

In Asia the Church is often recognized as a community of compassion. Authentic disciples of Christ seek solidarity with people and walk with them in compassion as Jesus himself has done. This has high value for contemporary evangelizers.

Missioners today see themselves as authentically cooperating in the apostolates of the local Church in an auxiliary role. At the same time, mission societies desire to transmit their mission charism and mission enthusiasm to the local Church. Missioners seek to be in cooperative collaboration with other missionary groups and local Churches.

In today's world, an openness to doing mission in new ways, both by lifestyle and by apostolic work, is an important value. Missioners seek to concretize this creativity in new apostolates and in new forms of faith witness.

As has been the hallmark of authentic mission through the centuries, missioners continue their openness and willingness to invest time and energy in acculturation: learning difficult languages, struggling with making oneself and one's vocation understood, and genuinely adapting to a variety of cultures.

Again, in harmony with the best efforts in the mission tradition, missioners approach people's cultures and religions with a clear sense of humility. In recent times this has been demanded more, particularly as one recognizes the greatness of ancient world religions and as one accepts the powerlessness that all missionaries experience in countries where Catholics are an extreme minority.

A final value emerging from missionaries' experience is the exploration of new, inclusive structures of governance. Emphasis on the ecclesial and community aspects of team work as well as consensus and full participation in mission life are seen to be life-giving for all participants. Missioners remain open to exploring new structures that place them more at the service of people and effective mission.

THEOLOGICAL SYNTHESIS

Carrying the inductive theological method forward one more step, Maryknollers in Asia identify three key themes among many in their theology of mission. Their reflections have been greatly enriched by Pope John Paul II's recent Mission Encyclical *Redemptoris Missio*. This document gives priority to mission *ad gentes*. Geographically, this refers primarily to Asia; it is important to place emphasis on evangelization among those of other belief systems. In understanding their task well, Asian Maryknollers concentrate on three theological themes drawn from recent Church documents.

The first theme focuses on the description of evangelization found in Pope Paul VI's Apostolic Exhortation *Evangelii Nuntiandi*; it is a workable description of the missioner's task in Asia. Quoting Pope Paul, missioners accept that "evangelizing means bringing the Good News into all strata of humanity and through its influence, transforming humanity from within and making it new" (EN 18). This comprehensive holistic vision of evangelization is particularly applicable in the Asia-Pacific context.

Secondly, the missioners in Asia also note that a wide vision of evangelization is now found in the consciousness of the Church. Five principal elements of the Church's mission are repeatedly outlined by local, area (FABC), and theological documents from the universal Church. These five elements, taken together, form what is known as "integral evangelization." These key dimensions are:

a. Presence and Witness of Life
b. Social Development and Human Liberation
c. Interreligious Dialogue and Inculturation
d. Explicit Gospel Proclamation and Catechesis
e. Liturgical Life, Prayer, and Contemplation

All these elements are integral parts of the Church's total mission of evangelization. This view sees mission and evangelization holistically. It follows the example of Jesus himself, who lived this comprehensive vision of mission in witness, in deeds, in dialogue, in preaching, and in prayer. This vision seeks to link solid missiology with foundational ecclesiology and Christology.

The third theological theme particularly apropos in an Asian context is the key role of dialogue. The Federation of Asian Bishops' Conferences has repeatedly stressed this key attitude and approach in the Asian context. Missioners are aware that they engage in dialogue in various forms. Four forms of dialogue consistently recognized in Church documents are:

a. *The Dialogue of Life* (where people strive to live in an open and neighborly spirit, sharing their joys and sorrows, their human problems and preoccupations);
b. *The Dialogue of Action* (in which Christians and others collaborate for the integral development and liberation of people);
c. *The Dialogue of Theological Exchange* (where specialists seek to deepen their understanding of their respective religious heritages and to appreciate each other's spiritual values);
d. *The Dialogue of Religious Experience* (where persons, rooted in their own religious traditions, share their spiritual riches, for instance, with regard to prayer and contemplation, faith and ways of searching for God or the Absolute).

DOING MISSION REMAINS

The three foregoing theological insights are helpful guidelines for the field missioner to engage in integral evangelization in Asia today. Although simply expressed, they capture some of the best mission thinking in the Church today. Maryknollers see themselves implementing the Church's vision of evangelization as they remain faithful to these three foundational missiological directions.

As the Maryknollers in the Asia-Pacific Area drew their reflection process to its logical conclusion, they focused once again on their active engagement in mission. The reflection process helped them see their experiences and the values that emerged from their various apostolates. They also recognized how they have a wide vision of evangelization, similar to that enunciated by Paul VI and John Paul II, and that their apostolates focused upon many of the various elements of integral evangelization. They feel constantly called to rethink their missionary engagement so as to address the situations and challenges of mission in the 1990s and beyond.

Since Maryknollers began work in Asia 75 years ago, they have been strong in implementing elements of proclamation, catechesis, and liturgical life. However, in their mission in Asia in the 1990s, missioners realize the need to work at becoming more proficient at other elements in evangelization viewed holistically. They commit themselves to witness of life, social development and human liberation, interreligious and intercultural dialogue, and prayer and contemplation. As missioners they realize that the various elements of integral evangelization will receive different emphasis in any given time, place, or context. All this apostolic endeavor is undertaken as a collaborative service with the local Churches.

Challenges emerge from a comprehensive reading of contemporary realities of the Asia-Pacific Area. Maryknollers recognize that certain factors will provide them challenges in the 1990s. They list a few. Political changes will affect mission work for better or for worse. This is true in Hong Kong after 1997, in the unstable situation in Cambodia, in the changes on the Korean peninsula, and in the opening of Vietnam. There is great economic, political, and social flux in Asian countries today. This has resulted in challenging situations like the mass movement of migrant workers and refugees as well as a growing spiritual poverty coming from the loss of traditional values.

Missioners see the rapid intensification of environmental problems. They also see that there is a pervasive revolution in technology in general, and in communications in particular. This has exploded throughout every corner of Asia in recent decades. Mission must address these situations.

Missioners face their own particular problems. Many foreign mission societies experience declining numbers and aging personnel. There is an uncertain future for personnel in several places due to the difficulty of obtaining visas. This results in a shortage of personnel and a lack of continuity in apostolates. In addition, mission societies seek clarification on how they may best use temporary associates in their collaboration in mission.

Looking forward to the coming years of mission in Asia, the Maryknollers identified some apostolates as having a high priority. Several of these apostolates could involve a common mission response and cooperative efforts across national boundaries. This requires wide collaborative efforts between the missionaries in the many Asia-Pacific countries where Maryknoll serves.

A key challenge within Asia today is the movement of workers and refugees. Maryknollers admit that almost all countries in Asia are affected by this reality. There are those countries where people leave and those to which people come. This phenomenon of migration of people offers many avenues of evangelization.

It is hoped that the faith witness of Catholic migrants in countries where Catholics are few would be an effective witness. Seeking a true dialogue of life, action, and religious experience can enable this witness. A missionary role would be to call the receiving country to accountability in meeting the human needs of the migrants, who are often subject to exploitation. In addition, missionaries can call the home countries to strive to alleviate the conditions which cause or force this migration.

There can be cooperation between the "sending" and "receiving" countries in caring for the needs of the migrant workers. This reality also provides an opportunity to facilitate dialogue with peoples of diverse religious traditions, since the economic migrants of Asia frequently cross religious boundaries as they move from one country to another. This is an opportunity to promote the dialogue of life in action.

Another distinct apostolate for the coming years in mission is continuous collaboration with the local Churches. This work should have some of the following characteristics. It should promote and enable *ad gentes* mission by the local Church. It should facilitate the formation of parish communities into missionary communities that engage in all the elements of integral evangelization. Collaborating with the local Church can also mean that missioners would serve by engaging in ministries/services that the local Church is not presently equipped to maintain.

Missioners in the 1990s would seek to emphasize the social development and human liberation elements of integral evangelization. They can address unhealthy and destructive social trends such as consumerism, environmental pollution, militarism, and sexism. Missioners can work against the exploitation of women and youth. They understand how this suffering is often related to international tourism and migrant labor. Missioners have an opportunity to be in the forefront of AIDS education and the pastoral care of AIDS patients.

In harmony with its 75-year tradition in Asia, Maryknoll specifically seeks continued involvement in China and expresses its openness to new missionary situations elsewhere (e.g. Cambodia and Vietnam).

Being in mission during the closing years of this millennium would see missioners renewing their efforts at interreligious dialogue and inculturation. Contemplation and development of houses of prayer and reflection would be a creative avenue so that the Christian tradition can interact with the Buddhist/Hindu/Muslim traditions of prayer and contemplation.

Although initial projects have been undertaken, missioners must renew their efforts to effectively use the means of mass communication for evangelization. Cooperation with existing media efforts, seeking collaboration from the media, using videos and printed materials, and computer networking would all be new avenues for missionary evangelization in Asia in the 1990s.

CONCLUDING SYNTHESIS

This presentation has been a lengthy narration of an extended process of pastoral-theological reflection. It has been at the service of mission; it has unfolded in several stages. Readers will recall that this piece presented: (i) the Asia-Pacific *context* of mission; (ii) the *experience* of missioners in ten countries; (iii) the missionary *values* directly emerging from missioners' experience; (iv) a brief *theological synthesis* of key missiological insights; (v) a call to *continued involvement* in the task of foreign mission.

One could legitimately note that this reflection process has come full circle: it originated in the lived faith and experience of missioners;

it concludes with a call to renewed involvement in direct mission and evangelization. This presentation reflects the fact that missioners are engaged people at every level of the missionary enterprise; for them mission is a life-giving vocation; for the missionary, to live is to evangelize, to live is to be in mission.

Maryknollers do not have the illusion that they possess a monopoly on mission; mission is God's project, it is always an "ecclesial act" (EN 60). Yet, the 75 years of Maryknoll's Asia-Pacific mission experience contain valuable insights for the wider Church and other mission societies. This is the spirit in which these reflections are presented and shared.

Bishop James Anthony Walsh, Maryknoll's co-founder and the very first Maryknoller to enter China, gave some wise advice to seminarians and fellow Maryknollers about relating to local Churches and other missionary societies. He frequently repeated: "BE BIG: bigger than your mission – bigger than your Society, as big as the Church." This same spirit of generosity and magnanimity motivates this presentation and sharing of Maryknoll's mission experience for the wider Church and missionary world. May these reflections serve mission, the Church, the Gospel, and the Kingdom.

Joining Mission to Ministry

In the wake of the renewal of the Church initiated by Pope John XXIII's call for *aggiornamento*, various new ministry forms have emerged in the Church. This phenomenon has developed within diverse local Church settings around the world – whether in Asia, Latin America, or in Africa, in technological or developing countries, whether Christians are in the minority or in the majority. Renewal in ministry is a clear sign of the Spirit breathing new life and dynamism into the Christian community.

The local Churches in Asia quickly perceived the action of the Spirit in renewing ministry; together they sponsored the progressive "Asian Colloquium on Ministries in the Church" (Hong Kong, 1977). Two years later at the "International Congress on Mission" (Manila, 1979), an entire workshop was given over to exploring ministries within local communities. This momentum and evolution in ministry continues to grow as local Churches everywhere mature and truly become "the acting subject of mission" (FABC V, 1990).

Ministry never functions in isolation or in a vacuum. Everyone called to ministry struggles to respond to the social, cultural, political, economic, as well as religious needs of the local community. A long series of questions accompanies the Church and her ministers: What should the Church be in the changing Asian world marked by much poverty, suffering and injustice? How does the minority Asian Church address the followers of Buddhism, Hinduism, and Islam? How do Church workers dialogue with Asia's many cultures, religions, and peoples?

These are but a small sampling of the burning questions which face those called to ministry today; they need serious attention by committed ministers. A fine resource for exploring one's identity in ministry is the mission encyclical by Pope John Paul II: *Redemptoris Missio* (On the Permanent Validity of the Church's Missionary Mandate).

If one is searching for concrete and specific answers to questions similar to those noted earlier, the mission encyclical will disappoint. However, if one desires to explore a paradigm for dynamic, persevering ministry, then one will discover rich resources in this document. Seeking to enhance all ministers' identity and enthusiasm (so as to face difficult concrete challenges), this piece explores (through key encyclical insights) core elements of the contemporary call to Christian ministry.

MYSTERY

The origins of ministry are found in mystery *(mysterion)*, understood in the Pauline sense as God's universal loving plan of salvation for the entire world. God loves all peoples, desiring everyone to be saved and to come to know the truth (I Tim. 2:4). The goal of ministry, then, is to serve the unfolding of this wonderful design God has for people (RM 41).

Further exploration into the *mysterion*-theology of St. Paul helps anchor the foundations of ministry. Paul is absolutely certain that God has a wonderful, marvelous vision of salvation for the whole world. His letter to the Ephesians convincingly – almost mystically – explains how "God has given us the wisdom to understand fully the mystery" (1:9), "the mysterious design which for ages was hidden in God" (3:9).

Pauline reflection on God's loving plan of salvation *(mysterion)* synthesizes his belief that this design has been fully revealed in Christ the Savior and will be recapitulated in Christ at the end of time (RM 4, 5, 41, 44). This manifestation is focused on salvation, not condemnation or judgment, and is open to all peoples (RM 55). It unfolds in stages: God, Jesus, Spirit, Church, world; humanity's response is faith or personal appropriation of the *mysterion* (RM 6, 9, 11).

Paul is a true minister of the Good News, a missionary par excellence because he believed, lived, prayed, labored, and suffered so that God's loving plan for the redemption of humanity would be known and graciously received. Obviously, Paul's missionary commitment had the "*mysterion*-encounter" as its central driving force.

Paul clearly recognized himself as a chosen minister and servant of the Gospel. (Rom. 1:1-6; I Cor. 4:1; 15:9-11; Eph. 3:1-21; Col. 1:24-29). It might be stated that this awareness engulfed and consumed Paul; for him life or death no longer mattered (Rom. 14:8); he gloried in giving his life for Christ (II Tim. 4:6). He emphatically declared: "Woe to me if I do not preach the Gospel" (I Cor. 9:16 and RM 1).

MEDITATION

Because all ministry flows from God's loving plan of salvation *(mysterion)*, the minister necessarily seeks to be deeply rooted in this mystery. There simply is no other foundation for all that one does. "Meditation" is a possible manner of expressing the "rooting-process" whereby the Christian minister seeks to discover God's constant loving presence in the depths of the soul.

A meditative awareness or consciousness should flow through the various actions of life (prayer, scripture-reading, experience, reflection, service); it should serve as a running thread and connecting bond in all the various activities of the day, through the different periods and stages of life. Such an uninterrupted and continuous flow will make the minister's whole life a prayer and a state of meditation/contemplation. In a word, the person in ministry must strive to develop a deep "*mysterion*-consciousness."

This present discussion focuses attention on the minister's need of a spirituality. If the previous section (MYSTERY) outlined God's plan of salvation in Pauline categories, this section (MEDITATION) emphasizes the personal appropriation and integration of the *mysterion* into our lives, activities, our very consciousness. The mission encyclical contains rich material for enhancing a spirituality of ministry.

In particular, two chapters of *Redemptoris Missio* treat *Spirit*-uality. The third chapter presents "The Holy Spirit, the Principal Agent of Mission"; chapter eight is entitled: "Mission Spirituality." All spirituality centers on God's action in, with, and through the minister; ministry is

"God's work," "the work of the Spirit"; it is not based "on human abilities but on the power of the Risen Lord" (RM 23, 24).

In the profoundly reflective chapter on the Spirit, one finds some of the most creative insights of the encyclical. Both the opening and closing paragraphs frame the discussion by asserting that "the principal agent of the whole Church's mission" is the Holy Spirit (RM 21, cf. 30). All evangelizers, like Christ himself, experience *"a sending forth in the Spirit"* (RM 22). As Gospel ministers, "we are missionaries above all because of *what we are* as a Church whose innermost life is unity in love, even before we become missionaries *in word or deed"* (RM 23).

The Spirit's action is both within and beyond the bounds of the Church. The encyclical notes that "the Spirit's presence and activity affect not only individuals but also society and history, peoples, cultures and religions.... The Spirit of God with marvelous foresight directs the course of the ages and renews the face of the earth.... We are obliged to hold that the Holy Spirit offers everyone the possibility of sharing in the Paschal Mystery in a manner known to God" (RM 28).

Proceeding to chapter eight (entitled: "Missionary Spirituality"), one finds several precious pearls for those in ministry. Spirituality demands "a life of complete docility to the Spirit" (87), "intimate communion with Christ" (88), and following Jesus "along the path of suffering and humiliation" (87). The minister must be "a person of charity" who practices "love without exclusion or partiality" (89). One must respond to "the universal call to holiness" and become "a person of the Beatitudes" (90).

Scattered at various points in the mission encyclical one finds two themes related directly to a spirituality for ministry: Conversion and Eucharist. Jesus invites his co-workers "to faith, conversion and the desire for forgiveness" (14). For the minister, "conversion is expressed in faith which is total and radical, and which neither limits nor hinders God's gift" (46). "We cannot preach conversion unless we ourselves are converted anew every day" (47). As ministers and disciples, all are called "to carry out a sincere review of their lives regarding their solidarity with the poor" (60); "we should reassess our own way of living" (81); "Fight hunger by changing your lifestyle" (59).

Vatican II has noted that the Eucharist is the source and summit of the Christian life; Eucharist is eminently central for the minister. One clear purpose of ministry is "to bring people together in hearing the Gospel, in fraternal communion, in prayer and in the Eucharist (26).

The early Church always sent forth its new ministers in the context of the Eucharist (Acts 13:1-4). The popular word that Catholics use today for Eucharist is "mass"; the words for both mission *(missio)* and mass *(missa)* derive from the same source *(mittere)*; Eucharist always empowers us for ministry and mission.

MINISTRY

Perceiving one's call to active ministry within the Church and to service of the Christian people is a gradual growth process. The call to ministry emerges into consciousness and seeks a definite commitment as one meditates on one's role in the loving plan of God. Only a life of faith and prayer (MEDITATION) leads one to personally experience God's love and plan of salvation *(mysterion)*; it is precisely in this process that ministry becomes a personalized invitation for the mature Christian. In a word, MEDITATION on the MYSTERY is the only means to discern one's call to MINISTRY.

For a deeper understanding of ministry as "faith-service," one can profitably open the pages of *Redemptoris Missio*. The encyclical straightforwardly asserts: *"Mission* [ministry] *is an issue of faith"* (11). Without faith nothing will progress. The Church and her members – even those in ministry – will accomplish little unless their lives and apostolates are rooted in living faith.

John Paul II is a public witness to faith in Jesus. He lives what he challenges others to do. He notes: "From the beginning of my Pontificate I have chosen to travel to the ends of the earth" (1). These frequent and often grueling trips are "journeys of faith... for evangelical proclamation in spreading the Gospel" (63). *"Faith is strengthened when it is given to others"* (2).

Ministry always connotes service of others; it is manifested in a variety of forms and apostolates. The Church's various ministries seek to reach the total person within community. Here again, the mission encyclical offers helpful insights.

Two words capture John Paul II's comprehensive vision of ministry, "integral evangelization." Briefly, this means that ministry, evangelization and salvation are best viewed in a holistic fashion. In the Pope's words, "Jesus came to bring integral salvation, one which embraces the whole person" (11). "Evangelical witness... is directed towards integral human development" (42). In short, contemporary ministry develops the whole person and society. It touches the social and cultural, political and economic, historical and religious dimensions of life – all from the perspective of faith.

Key dimensions of integral ministry and evangelization are: the witness of Christian living (42), the service of humanity (58-60), inculturation and interreligious dialogue (52-54, 55-57), explicit Gospel proclamation (44-45), and sacramental-liturgical-ecclesial life (46-49). The totality of Christian ministry combines all these elements. They form the Church's total program of holistic evangelization; they follow the example of Jesus who lived ministry in silence and reflection, in action and service, in dialogue and outreach, in teaching and proclamation, as well as in prayer and contemplation. This is ministry; this is authentic "faith-service"!

MISSION

A stark question must be posed: Is it possible to have an authentic program of ministry without a vibrant sense of mission? Some may try to propose and defend such a possibility through rationalization. Yet, in the considered opinion of this author: ministry without a missionary dynamism and perspective can quickly degenerate into parochialism or provincialism. Promoting mission awareness one of the most urgent challenges facing all local Churches today!

The Second Vatican Council places mission and evangelization at the center of the Church: "The pilgrim Church is missionary by her very nature" (AG 2). Pope Paul VI spoke with deep conviction: "We wish to confirm once more that the task of evangelizing all peoples constitutes the essential mission of the Church.... Evangelizing is in fact the grace and vocation proper to the Church, her deepest identity. She exists in order to evangelize... " (EN 14).

What meaning does the imperative of evangelization have for the Church? She must become a living proclamation of the *mysterion* – God's loving design of universal salvation. Only in this way does the Church as the community of Jesus' disciples realize her "deepest identity" and "her very nature." She is called to be always and everywhere "the universal sacrament of salvation" (LG 48; AG 1). For her, to live is to evangelize! A non-missionary Church is impossible; it is self-contradictory. Animation and rededication are necessary, because Christians "are faithful to the nature of the Church to the degree that we love and sincerely promote her missionary activity" (EE 2).

Pope John Paul II is deeply concerned about the *"urgency of missionary activity"* (1); his concern precipitated the writing of an encyclical. He notes that "missionary activity specifically directed 'to the nations' appears to be waning." This fact "must arouse concern among all who believe in Christ [because] in the Church's history, missionary drive has always been a sign of vitality, just as its lessening is a sign of a crisis of faith" (2).

The Pope seeks the help of all – especially those in ministry – to promote "a new missionary age" (92), "a new springtime for the Gospel" (86), "a fresh impulse to missionary activity" (2). He senses "the moment has come to commit all of the Church's energies to a new evangelization" (3).

Such renewed commitment to mission is probably a key path for deepening the faith commitment of local Churches and ministers everywhere. Mission awareness is both a goal and crowning achievement of effective ministry. It remains a paradoxical truth that the home Church/parish is strengthened when it sends forth missioners – even out of an insufficient supply of personnel. God's ways are so often not our ways!

THE MINISTRY SPIRAL

This chapter has sought to capture and elucidate those key elements which are essential for effective ministry in the Church. One could term it the "4-M approach": MYSTERY, MEDITATION, MINISTRY, and MISSION. Each element builds upon and reinforces the other; if any dimension is lost or under-emphasized, ministry automatically suffers.

As a spiral, this approach to ministry must revolve – moving God's people, the Church, forward. At times, one dimension of the cycle may be more visible than another; yet, the spiral remains complete; all four Ms are important and essential.

Employing the "spiral of ministry" image, one could propose additional supports for this paradigm. Two central items (two more Ms) are the *Mass* (Eucharist) and *Mary* (Model of Discipleship and Ministry);

both dimensions greatly enhance the spiritual life of those called to ministry.

Permit one final suggestion: consider reading again and meditating on *Redemptoris Missio* in its entirety; your motivation for ministry will most certainly be enriched!

Guiding Vocation Recruitment in Mission

In the field of mission today a blunt and sensitive question must be raised: "Are we witnessing *vocation piracy* in some of the young, vibrant Churches in Africa, Asia, and Latin America"? This provocative question arises because of certain practices which, unfortunately, continue within some sectors of the Church. One short, true example will illustrate the point clearly.

Early in 1990 an American religious, whose society is of Italian origin, arrives in an Asian country. The individual has never before been on a mission assignment. A location is established in an affluent section of the capital city; vocation recruitment and acceptance begin.

Other missionaries with many decades of service to the local Church, as well as many of the diocesan/indigenous clergy and religious, react with distaste. Some of their vocation prospects and sincere youth are being siphoned off by this latest arrival. Everyone would agree that the tension and competition created in this situation are unfortunate. What can be done?

There is no "magic formula" for settling this sticky problem. Who should take the initiative? How can the misguided enthusiasm of the new recruiter be contained? Is it responsible just to let the problem simmer and hope for the best? Is it in the sincere interest of mission, the local Church as well as mission societies to speak openly of the problem? The list of unanswered questions is lengthy.

This author, a veteran missionary, believes that the problem should be aired frankly and directly. My approach is not accusatory, not filled with rivalry, not seeking self-justification. The sincere promotion of "professional approaches to mission and vocation recruitment" motivates this brief piece.

In addressing the question at hand, this chapter presents points for reflection from three perspectives: (a) Guidelines for Mission Societies drawn from overseas mission experience; (b) Qualities of Church Workers recommend by the Federation of Asian Bishops' Conferences; and, (c) a Pastoral Letter which deals with "Establishing Houses of Religious Institutes and Recruiting Vocations" by Jaime Cardinal Sin of Manila.

Missionaries, local clergy, and religious recruiters need assistance as they approach the vocation question; it is a sensitive topic. Thus, these guidelines need wide dissemination so as to reduce conflicts within the local Church and among religious. Healthy mission activity, with the goal of building up a truly local Church, remains the focus for presenting the following guidelines

GUIDELINES FOR MISSION SOCIETIES

(1) It must be the primary focus of missionaries to serve in, through and with the local Church; this statement reflects solid current missiological thinking.

(2) Upon first arrival, missionaries should normally undertake an extended period of "apostolic inactivity" (8-24 months) to learn the language and begin their lifelong acculturation process.

(3) Newly arrived missionaries should seek the advice and wisdom of Church personnel who have experience and lengthy service in the country; they need a "cultural advisor" to continually guide them.

(4) International societies should serve within the local Church for a minimum of 7-10 years before accepting local candidates into their religious families. In short, they should give service and till the soil before picking fruit.

(5) Preservation of a religious society that is aging or dying in the West must never be the motivation for opening houses in countries where "vocations are plentiful."

(6)   Missionaries would do well to train some of their own expatriate personnel in the countries where they work; these people could, in turn, be "inculturated" formation personnel – if and when the society decides to accept local applicants.

(7)   Promises of training and education abroad should never be offered or used as enticements to attract prospective applicants; such hopes become nearly irresistible temptations for young people in developing countries. This confuses the true vocational calling and can result in the "cultural alienation" of a candidate.

(8)   Societies should consider whether it is better to encourage prospective applicants to enter groups (diocesan or religious) already established in the country, to found a separate society particularly fitted to the local needs, or to accept applicants into their own society. This decision should not be made outside the local Church (e.g. in a generalate in Rome or the U.S.A.).

(9)   Newly arrived religious societies must sensitively avoid wooing or even "stealing" prospective applicants from other religious/diocesan groups who have cultivated vocations through extended witness and service in the country.

(10)   Religious and missionaries must be extremely alert and cognizant of the situation and sensibilities of the local Church; otherwise, all missionaries (mission itself) can be placed in a bad light because of the attitude and mistakes of a few foreign missionaries.

These ten points, expressing the convictions and experience of many missionaries, can be complemented by suggestions of the Federation of Asian Bishops' Conferences (FABC). Nearly a decade ago, they composed a 25-point list of the qualities of personnel needed by the local Churches of Asia. Again, it goes without saying, missionaries must heed with intent sensitivity the expressed wishes of the local Church they come to accompany through service.

QUALITIES OF CHURCH WORKERS

As noted by the FABC, the churches of Asia (Africa/Latin America) need workers who:

(1) Are up-to-date with post-Vatican II theology.

(2)   Are able to engage in interreligious dialogue.

(3)   Know and appreciate Asian philosophies, religions, traditions, and ideological currents.

(4)   Are convinced of the need for the Church to go out to evangelize but understand what this means today in diverse circumstances.

(5)   Are able to contribute to the inculturation of doctrine, practice, etc., of the Church.

(6)   Are in favor of dialogue within the Church and will exercise leadership as service and foster coresponsibility, dialogue and participation in the Church.

(7)   Know how to foster Christian community growth in Small Christian Communities, parishes and churches.

(8)   Can function well in Christian ecumenical collaboration and dialogue.

(9)   Are men and women of prayer and contemplation who seek meaning in the signs of the times.

(10)   Can teach prayer and spiritual growth to individuals and communities – prayer which is inculturated.

(11)   Can aid the vital celebration of sacraments.

(12)   Are capable of prayerful contextualized theological reflection at different levels.

(13)   Will incorporate the social teaching of the Church at all levels of Christian instruction.

(14)   Wish to live a life not distant from the poor but in ongoing dialogue with the poor.

(15)   Wish to and can engage in work with the people for justice, development and liberation through conscientization and by accompanying them with the Gospel in their action on behalf of justice, all the time avoiding clericalism.

(16)   As teachers will involve students in social orientation and spiritual leadership.

(17)   Have grasped to a useful extent the contribution of behavioral and social sciences for personal, group, and social development.

(18)   Are able to understand the situation of youth and work effectively with or for the mass of young people in this part of the world.

(19)   Are able to help people in the current confusions of cultural change, secularization, industrialization, urbanization, etc.

(20)   Appreciate the role of women in the Church.

(21)   Will be clearly aware of the stresses on family life and know some approaches towards helping family life.

(22)   Appreciate the role of mass and group media evangelization, education, and development together with media's sometimes more negative effects and the ways of reducing these effects.

(23)   Have at least fundamental skills in the use of media.

(24)   Will be concerned to build up creatively new ministries in the Church and give proper place to the growth of lay responsibility.

(25)   Are desirous of learning from the other Catholic Churches of Asia/Africa/Latin America and to cooperate with them.

One sincerely prays that the Lord of the Harvest and the Owner of the Vineyard enriches the local Churches of Asia, Africa, and Latin America with both indigenous and missionary personnel possessing these needed qualities for authentic service.

PASTORAL LETTER

On April 10, 1990 Jaime Cardinal Sin as Archbishop of Manila issued a pastoral letter entitled *Establishing Houses of Religious Institutes and Recruiting Vocations.* This document provides helpful theology and guidelines for missionaries and local Churches worldwide. The letter is as follows:

(1)   Since the Second Vatican Council a fresh awareness has sprung up that within the Christian Community everyone is called to holiness, whether belonging to the hierarchy or to the lay faithful. This holiness is expressed in many ways, but appears in a very special way in the practice of the evangelical counsels, undertaken by many either privately or in Church-approved Institutes of Religious Life (*De Ecclesia*, Ch. 5, No. 39).

(2)   A further thought on this call to holiness by all was worked out by the Synod of Bishops of 1987 on the Vocation and Mission of the lay faithful. Holiness for all is more than a simple moral exhortation. It is an undeniable requirement arising from the mystery of the Church. Every Christian is charged to strive after the perfection of charity. By this they

will be recognized as true disciples of Christ (*Christifidelis Laici*, No. 16).

(3) Linked to the duty of every baptized Christian to strive after holiness is the ecclesiology of Communion, proposed by the Second Vatican Council and recalled by the 1985 Extraordinary Synod of Bishops, and which integrates the central content of the "mystery" which is the divine plan for the salvation of humankind. At one and the same time this ecclesial communion is characterized by the diversity and complementarity of vocations and states of life, of ministries, of charisms and responsibilities (*Christifidelis Laici*, Nos. 19, 20).

(4) Members of Religious Institutes will have to review their commitment, therefore, to holiness and apostolic works as incentives to growth of the Church as *Communio*. Each Institute is a gift of God authenticated by the hierarchy, who is charged to accompany and encourage the Institute in its fidelity to its founding gift (cf. *Document CRIS*, May 31, 1983, Nos. 40-42).

(5) The people of God who are the Archdiocese of Manila, have been immensely enriched by the fruits of holiness emanating from the wide variety of Religious Institutes which have their communities within the boundaries of the Archdiocese. More than any other Diocese in the country, the Manila Archdiocese has been blessed by a great diversity, yet complementarity of Institutes of Religious Life.

Within the last ten years more than eighty new congregations of women have established themselves in the Philippines and most of them have a house in Manila.

(6) In view of the above, the Archdiocese of Manila, charged with the responsibility to coordinate all gifts and ministries towards the building up of the People of God, deems it opportune to declare and ordain the following:

a. Prior to establishing a House of a Religious Institute within the Archdiocese of Manila, the consent of the Archbishop in writing is required in compliance with Canon 609. In asking for this permission from the Archbishop, the Institute must clearly state the purpose of establishing its Community in the Archdiocese, and explain how it envisions its charisms and apostolate to contribute to the building up of God's people in Manila.

b. In the case of Religious Institutes coming from abroad and making their first foundation in the Archdiocese of Manila, it will be for the good of those Institutes as well as out of respect for the local Church, to avoid any form of recruitment within their first five years in the country. Religious Institutes have the full right to foster vocations for themselves and seek candidates, but with due prudence and according to the norms of the Holy See and the local bishop (*Decree on Religious Life*, No.24).

The reason for this restriction is that it takes time to know the candidates and assess their cultural and academic background, their religious disposition and psychological maturity. To discern a vocation is a work of love, respecting each person who needs time for making a mature response.

The above is to take effect as of May 1, 1990.

ANIMATION FOR MISSION

Recently John Paul II gave a very welcomed gift to the Church and to missionaries in particular: his mission encyclical *Redemptoris Missio*. Its central theme focused on "the urgency of missionary activity" (1). Concretely implementing this papal exhortation necessarily involves recruiting and animating personnel into mission; to this end, chapter six of the encyclical dwells on "Leaders and Workers in the Missionary Apostolate" (61-76). Cooperation and collaboration are the operative principles for motivating the entire Church and promoting a "New Springtime" in mission (86).

Mission institutes, bishops, diocesan and religious priests, as well as sisters and pastoral agents must all harmoniously focus their energies on seeking laborers for the vast harvest (Mt. 9:37-38). One must state emphatically that "*vocation skimming*" or "*vocation piracy*" should be assiduously avoided. Local Churches and religious societies are not to engage in anything that smacks of the "*numbers game*" in vocation recruitment; it is the Lord alone who will give the desired growth and increase (I Cor. 3:6).

John Paul II outlines his vision in this way: "Missionary personnel coming from other Churches and countries must work in communion with their local counterparts.... In particular, it falls to missionary personnel – in accordance with the directives of the Bishops and in cooperation with those responsible at the local level... to encourage a missionary sense within the particular Churches, so that pastoral concern will always be combined with concern for the mission *ad gentes*" (49).

The pope straightforwardly expresses his optimism: "I see the dawning of a new missionary age, which will become a radiant day bearing an abundant harvest, if all Christians, and missionaries and young Churches in particular, respond with generosity and holiness to the calls and challenges of our time (92).

Knowing Our Muslim Neighbors

If one sincerely wishes to approach another living faith tradition, it is best done from the perspective of a follower or believer of that religion. This is a basic ground rule for interreligious dialogue. In addition, the choice of descriptive language for any religion must reflect a sensitivity to people and their religious convictions.

In the Philippine (or Asian) context, the following suggestions are offered as "preferred" or "correct" terminology when speaking of Muslim neighbors and their Islamic faith.

— *Islam* is the name of the religion. Never use Mohammedanism, because it could imply that Muhammad founded Islam. Christianity is established upon Jesus the Christ; Islam is not "founded" by or upon Muhammad. He is the Prophet but is *not* divine.

— The person who adheres to Islam is a *Muslim*; one is not called a Moslem or Mohammedan. A Muslim is one who does *islam*, that is, submits to the will of Allah.

— The term *"Moro"* is used to refer to Muslim Filipinos. It has undergone an evolution in meaning and connotation. Originally, "Moro" came from the Latin *maurus* and was used by the Romans for the people of Mauretania in northwest Africa. Spaniards transformed it into "Moro" and applied it to the Muslim "Moors" (English) who ruled Spain. When Muslims were encountered in the Philippines, Spaniards quite naturally called them "Moros."

Unfortunately, the word "Moro" has frequently been used in a derogatory, pejorative sense. Mutually negative images of Muslims and Christians have been perpetuated by ignorance and prejudice.

In recent years, the Muslims of Mindanao and Sulu in the southern Philippines have proudly called themselves "Moro" to depict their identity as a people as well as their courageous gallantry by which they resisted both Spanish and American intrusions. "Moro" presently connotes a clear dignity and self-identity. Thus, it was used with pride in speaking of the Bangsa Moro people, the Moro National Liberation Front (MNLF), and the Moro Islamic Liberation Front (MILF).

— The scripture or sacred book of Muslims is the Qur'an (not Koran). It was revealed to Muhammad. It is incorrect to attribute authorship of the *Qur'an* to Muhammad. Whereas the Christian scriptures are "God's Word in human words," the Qur'an is the verbatim word or uncreated speech of Allah.

— A common misperception is the belief that all Muslims are Arabs and that all Arabs are Muslim. There are many Arabs who are Christians and followers of other faiths. The Philippines' closest neighbor is Indonesia and numerically it is the nation with the largest Muslim population in the world.

— *"Jihad"* is not literally translated as "holy war." In an Islamic faith perspective, it means "struggle for the cause of Allah" or "an extraordinary effort made for accomplishing God's purposes in the world." Thus, *"jihad"* may be used with political and social applications, but its primary meaning is a religious one.

— The phenomenon of "folk Christianity" or popular religiosity is well known in the Philippines. Among Filipino Muslims, there is also "folk Islam." There are both nominal Christians and nominal Muslims, but it is probably true that the majority of nominal Muslims take their faith more seriously than do the majority of nominal Christians.

— The Second Vatican Council spoke very respectfully about the followers of the Prophet Muhammad:

Upon the Muslims, too, the Church looks with esteem. They adore one God, living and enduring, merciful and all-powerful, Maker of heaven and earth and Speaker to all. They strive to submit wholeheartedly, even to His inscrutable decrees, just as did Abraham, with whom the Islamic faith is pleased to associate itself. Though they do not acknowledge Jesus as God, they revere Him as a prophet. They also honor Mary, His virgin mother; at times they call on her, too, with devotion. In addition, they await the day of judgment when God will give each one his due after raising him up. Consequently, they prize the moral life, and give worship to God especially through prayer, almsgiving, and fasting.

Although in the course of the centuries many quarrels and hostilities have arisen between Christians and Muslims, this most sacred Synod urges all to forget the past and to strive sincerely for mutual understanding. On behalf of all humanity, let them make common cause of safeguarding and fostering social justice, moral values, peace, and freedom (NA 3).

— Pope John Paul II recently addressed the following words to the bishops of the Visayas and Mindanao in the Philippines:

In many of your dioceses the Catholic faithful live side by side with members of the Muslim faith. Here and there certain tensions have arisen in the area of political aspirations. Yet, on the basis of the common bond of faith in the Most High God and out of respect for one of the world's great religious traditions, your local Churches are actively maintaining good relations with the Muslim community and are already offering a fruitful collaboration and service in educational and social activities. It is important to make further progress along this path of mutual understanding and harmony.

I would repeat to the Church in the Philippines what I said to a gathering of Muslim young people during my recent visit to Morocco: "Dialogue between Christians and Muslims is today more necessary than ever.... I believe that we, Christians and Muslims, must recognize with joy the religious values that we have in common, and give thanks to God for this fact.... I believe that, today, God invites us *to change our old practices.* We must respect each other, and also we must stimulate each other in good works on the path of God (AAS 78:271).

Reflective Vignettes

Allowing God to be God

Pope John Paul II's mission encyclical urging a renewal of Catholic missionary efforts arrived precisely when the world most desperately needed a message of hope and Good News. It is coincidental but not insignificant that the encyclical was released the same week of January, 1991 as the outbreak of the war in the Persian Gulf.

The war brought countless tragedies for both sides. As feared, the opposing forces often vilified each other's traditions, cultures, and religions. What was a political and economic conflict came to be portrayed, at times, in religious overtones – even by persons (Jews, Muslims and Christians) who consider themselves religious. The mission encyclical condemns prejudicial attitudes of intolerance among believers of different faiths; in fact, the Pope addresses them as "our brothers and sisters of other religions" and asserts that "interreligious dialogue is part of the Church's evangelizing mission" (RM 55).

As an American missionary with over 20 years' experience living in a Muslim culture, I am profoundly grateful to the Pope for his teaching on this subject. The years I spent working on the island of Mindanao in southern Philippines and in Bangladesh have completely changed my outlook on life and faith. Now, when I approach God in prayer, I do it in a Christian-Muslim manner. Islamic insights have expanded my understanding of God. My "hybrid" spirituality is, in fact, a deeper Christian experience.

Missionaries often develop dual personalities; their psychological makeup is shaped by their culture-by-birth as well as their culture-by-adoption. They benefit from being able to choose the best elements of both cultural worlds.

While centered in Christ, missioners always integrate insights of other religious traditions within their own faith life. Nothing holy in other religions is rejected, because as the encyclical acknowledges, these faiths reflect rays of God's truth. Thus, missionaries are called to promote interfaith harmony and "the elimination of prejudice, intolerance and misunderstandings" (RM 56).

In my "Christian-Islamic" approach to God, I accept that the divine transcends my inadequate human awareness and knowledge. This realization keeps our relationship in balance: God is the Almighty and I am a creature or servant within a covenant of loving trust. In short, I freely allow God to be God.

As a missioner, I know that God rules, guides and directs my life. I willingly offer my total cooperation, and intelligently place myself at God's service. I voluntarily humble myself "under the mighty hand of God" (I Pt. 5:6). The obligation to acknowledge God is at the heart of Muslim faith as well; all true religion is characterized by free and loving surrender.

There are many striking parallels between Islam and Christianity. Both religions counsel submission to God and cooperation with God's loving designs.

This same surrender is expressed in Ignatius of Loyola's Christian prayer, which echoes profound Islamic sentiments: "Take, O Lord, and receive all my liberty, my memory, my understanding and my entire will. Whatever I have or hold, you have given me; I restore it all to you and surrender it wholly to be governed by your will. Give me only your love and your grace, and I am rich enough and ask for nothing more."

Ignatius' prayer, which I memorized in elementary school and usually recite after receiving the Eucharist, has taken on a more profound meaning, precisely because of my appreciation of Islamic spirituality. Witnessing devout Muslims in submissive prayer is a summons to a deeper and more authentic commitment on my part.

A missioner's familiarity with and appreciation of the faith and sacred books of the world's great religions is an important element within one's own unique vocation. Paradoxically, not only have I found that my Christian faith has been enlightened and deepened through the Qur'an and Islamic insights, but I also hope that this experience has made me a more sensitive missionary to the Muslim community. The affirmation of reverence for all faiths and interreligious dialogue in the Pope's mission encyclical renews my enthusiasm to continue promoting Muslim-Christian harmony and world peace.

Bridging Muslims
and Christians

It is a sad story. The more than four hundred years of Christian-Muslim interaction in the Philippines have often been centuries of mutual suspicion, prejudice, and aggression. Yet, in spite of past hostilities, Catholics are urged by the Church today to promote a spirit of reconciliation with their Muslim neighbors. In the Virgin Mary, they can find one bridge to harmonious existence.

Another story is NOT a sad one. It took place last month in Manila while I was waiting in an office before formal business hours. There I had a fascinating conversation with a charming young lady.

Although presently employed in Manila, she originates from Jolo, southern Philippines. In the course of our friendly chat, she proudly told me how her name "Mary Ann" reflects her family which is part Muslim and part Christian.

She narrated her background: "When my parents were choosing my name, it was my Muslim grandfather who insisted on 'Mary' because of his admiration for Mary, the mother of Jesus the prophet. Furthermore, he urged that my second name would be 'Ann' in honor of Mary's mother. Thus, while acceding to my parents' decision that I would be baptized a Christian, he believed that my Muslim heritage would not be lost because of the name he had chosen for me." She concluded her story: "I'm very happy that my own name symbolizes who I am – both Christian and Muslim."

Catholics should be delighted to discover how much Christians and Muslims have in common. Reverence for Mary is a dominant element of Muslim-Christian mutuality, a source of unity and a key for superseding hostilities. Listen to the words of the Second Vatican Council on the proper attitude of Catholics toward their Muslim neighbors: "Although in the course of the centuries many quarrels and hostilities have arisen between Christians and Muslims, this most sacred Synod urges all to forget the past and to strive sincerely for mutual understanding. On behalf of all humanity, let them make common cause of safeguarding and fostering social justice, moral values, peace and freedom" (NA 3).

Most Christians are unaware of the reverence that Muslims have for Mary. Her name *(Maryam)* appears explicitly in the Qur'an 34 times. In 24 of these references, she is identified as the mother of Jesus *('Issa)*. One chapter of the Qur'an (Sura 19) is entitled *"Maryam"* and narrates events of the Annunciation and Jesus' birth. In addition, Muslims call Mary *Sitti Maryam*; *Sitti* is a term of endearment because of her privilege to be the mother of the prophet *'Issa*.

Muhammad's attitude toward Mary was always reverent and respectful. He spoke of her as a sign *(ayat)* for all creation and a model *(mathal)* for all believers. As the Qur'an notes (66:12), "she put her trust in the words of her Lord and believed in His Scriptures." The Prophet of Mecca saw Mary as a sign and model because she truly submitted *(Islam)* to the will of Allah/God. This same virtue of Mary is recorded by St. Luke: "Mary said: I am the servant of the Lord. Let it be done to me as you say" (1:38).

Another Marian parallel is found in both the Islamic and Christian faiths: Mary has a special dignity as one favored by God. The Qur'an (3:42) says: "Allah has chosen you, and made you pure, and exalted you above all women"; the Gospel of Luke (1:28, 42) states: "Hail, full of grace... blessed are you among women."

Catholics reverence Mary under several titles, one of which is "Our Lady of Fatima." Here one can discover an interesting Muslim-Christian bond. It is historical fact that the Muslims occupied Portugal for several centuries. At the time when they were driven out, the last Muslim ruler had a beautiful daughter named Fatima. A young Catholic man loved her and for him she stayed behind when the Muslims left. The husband was so much in love with her that he changed the town's name to Fatima. Thus, the very place where Our Lady appeared in 1917 bears an historical connection to Fatima, the favorite daughter of Muhammad. When commenting on this fact, Bishop Fulton J. Sheen once noted: "I believe that the Blessed Virgin chose to be known as 'Our Lady of Fatima' as a pledge and sign of hope to the Muslim people."

The Catholic Church sought to promote a new vision of human relationships at the Second Vatican Council; we read in its documents: "Upon the Muslims, too the Church looks with esteem" (NA 3). Yes, "the plan of salvation also includes those who acknowledge the Creator. In the first place among these there are the Muslims, who, professing to hold the faith of Abraham, along with us adore the one and merciful God, who on the last day will judge humanity" (LG 16).

Again, many Catholics will no doubt be surprised at the words of Vatican II which elaborate Muslim-Christian similarities; the Muslims "adore one God, living and enduring, merciful and all-powerful, Maker of heaven and earth and Speaker to all. They strive to submit whole-heartedly even to His inscrutable decrees, just as did Abraham, with whom the Islamic faith is pleased to associate itself. Though they do not acknowledge Jesus as God, they revere Him as a prophet. *They also honor Mary, his Virgin Mother: at times they call on her, too, with devotion*. In addition, they await the day of judgment when God will give each one his due after raising him up. Consequently, they prize the moral life, and give worship to God especially through prayer, almsgiving, and fasting" (emphasis added) (NA 3).

Statistically, by the year 2000 there will be more Muslims than Catholics in the world. The year 2000 is already near; according to demographers, it will see Muslims representing 19.2% of the world's population; Catholic Christians will be 18.7%. Realistically facing the peoples and religions of the world, the Church says that she "rejects nothing which is true and holy in these religions." Catholics are requested to "acknowledge, preserve, and promote the spiritual and moral goods found among these men" because these "often reflect a ray of that Truth which enlightens all" (NA 2).

The mission encyclical *Redemptoris Missio* reaffirms God's love and call for all peoples; God "does not fail to make himself present in many ways, not only to individuals but also to entire peoples through their spiritual riches, of which their religions are the main and essential expression" (RM 55).

A final story illustrates the reverence that Muslims in Mindanao, southern Philippines, have for Mary. In Zamboanga a Muslim high school student explained to his Jesuit teacher why he had missed a day of class: "Yesterday was the fiesta of the Virgin Mary, Nuestra Señora del Pilar. I visited her shrine at Fort Pilar to ask for help."

For Muslims and Christians alike in Zamboanga, Mary symbolizes that city's culture, history and destiny. A legend says that the city will be destroyed if the people stop praying to "Our Lady of the Pillar," a devotion that dates back to 1719. Many devout Muslims of Zamboanga are known to implore Mary's special protection during difficult times or before beginning their pilgrimage *(hajj)* to Mecca.

To be sure, Christians and Muslims are not in total agreement with all their beliefs about Mary. Yet, this should not prevent them from nurturing a deep and mutual reverence for Mary as "Our Lady" *(Sayidat)*. Beginning with common elements, these two great monotheistic religions can grow closer together; Mary can be one bridge to closer fellowship; Mary can become the "Common *Kaa'ba*" where Muslim and Christian clasp each other's hands in worship of the one, true God.

Becoming Eucharist

*During the meal Jesus took bread, blessed it,
broke it, and gave it to his disciples.*

Mt. 26:26

MYSTERY OF CHOOSING:

> Lord, you have taken and chosen me from among many,
> > called me to become your friend.
> Such a gracious choice convinces me of your love.
> > What a paradox! I belong to you!
> From the lowly and insignificant,
> > you freely selected me for service.
> "Lord, I am not worthy!"
> > Your love endures forever.

MIRACLE OF BLESSING:

> Lord, you have blessed me,
> > enriched me beyond measure.
> Family, vocation, community, mission:
> > all manifesting your generous, loving design.
> Your befriending Spirit gently directs my path,
> > opening new vistas and broader horizons.
> "Goodness and kindness follow me all the days of my life."
> > Your love endures forever.

PARADOX OF BREAKING:

Lord, why have you broken me?
    My limitations and failures weigh heavy upon me.
I attempt to speak – my tongue stutters;
    I struggle with community – I'm an outsider;
People see me as an enigma – I feel lonely;
    Problems and trials bruise and crush me.
"A broken, humbled heart, O Lord, you will not reject."
    Your love endures forever.

WONDER OF GIVING:

Lord, I experience fulfillment as
    your servant and herald.
Taken, blessed and broken,
    I am now shared and distributed,
May your people find nourishment, strength and consolation
    from my humble self-gift.
"Lord, you know all; you know that I love you."
    Your love endures forever.

Resources for Mission

Pope Paul VI's Gift
(December 8, 1975)

INTRODUCTION

1. Proclaiming the Gospel to the people of today is a service rendered to the Christian community and to the whole of humanity.

2. Three occasions prompt us to encourage our brothers and sisters in their mission as evangelizers:

a) The end of the Holy Year, during which time the Good News was proclaimed through two fundamental commands: "Put on the new self," (Eph. 4:24) and "Be reconciled to God" (II Cor. 5:20).

b) The tenth anniversary of the closing of the Second Vatican Council, a Council called to make the Church of the twentieth century better equipped and more ready to proclaim the Gospel to the people of the twentieth century.

c) One year after the Synod of Bishops on Evangelization.

3. This theme of evangelization has been stressed frequently in our time. It is only in the Christian message that humanity today can find

---

Caution: This is an unofficial summary of a 23,000 word papal document. In any formal discussion of evangelization, the full document should be at hand. This augmented synthesis is reprinted with permission.

the answer to key questions and the energy for commitment to human solidarity.

4. The 1974 Synod of Bishops on Evangelization posed three questions:

a) What has happened to that hidden energy of the Good News which is able to have such a powerful effect on the human conscience?

b) Is the evangelical force of the Gospels capable of transforming lives?

c) What methods should be followed to insure that the Gospel may have its proper impact?

5. The Church must reply to these three questions because the presentation of the Gospel message is not an optional contribution. It is the duty incumbent on Her by the command of the Lord Jesus, so that people can believe and be saved. This message is indeed necessary. It is unique. It is a question of the salvation of the human person.

Chapter One **FROM CHRIST THE EVANGELIZER TO THE EVANGELIZING CHURCH**

6. "I must proclaim the Good News of the Kingdom of God" without doubt has enormous consequences, for it sums up the whole mission of Jesus, for "That is what I was sent to do" (Lk. 4:43). "The Spirit of the Lord has been given to me, for He has anointed me. He has sent me to bring the good news to the poor" (Lk. 4:18).

7. Jesus Himself, the Good News of God (cf. Mk. 1:1) was the first and the greatest Evangelizer.

8. As an evangelizer, Christ first of all proclaims a kingdom, the Kingdom of God. This is so important that, by comparison, everything else in his preaching becomes "the rest," which is "given in addition."

9. The kernel and center of Christ's Good News is Salvation, this great gift of God which is liberation from everything that oppresses humanity, but which is, above all, liberation from sin and the evil one.

10. Each person can gain the Kingdom of God and Salvation through a total interior renewal, a radical conversion, a profound change of mind and heart.

11. Christ proclaims the Kingdom of God through His untiring preaching of the Word which has no equal elsewhere.

12. Christ manifests the divine content of this proclamation by innumerable signs and miracles, and more especially by His death, His Resurrection, and by sending the Holy Spirit.

13. Those who sincerely accept the Good News and who have been gathered by it into the community of salvation, can and must communicate and share it with others.

14. The Church exists in order to evangelize; that is to say, in order to preach and teach, to be the channel of the gift of grace, to reconcile sinners with God, and to perpetuate Christ's sacrifice in the Mass.

15. Anyone who re-reads the Gospel accounts of the origins of the Church sees that She is linked to evangelization in Her most intimate being:

- The Church is born of the evangelizing activity of Jesus and the Twelve.
- The Church, in turn, is sent by Jesus. The whole Church receives the mission to evangelize, and the work of each individual member is important to the whole.
- The Church is an evangelizer, but She begins by being evangelized Herself by constant conversion and renewal, in order to evangelize the world with credibility.
- The Church is the depository of the Good News to be proclaimed and She preserves it as a precious living heritage in order to communicate it.
- Having been sent and evangelized, the Church herself sends out evangelizers to pass the Gospel on with complete fidelity.

16. There is, therefore, a profound link between Christ, the Church and evangelization.

Chapter Two   WHAT IS EVANGELIZATION?

17. Any partial and fragmentary definition of evangelization which diminishes the richness, the complexity and the dynamism of evangelization impoverishes and distorts it.

18.   Evangelizing means bringing the Good News into all strata of humanity, and through its influence transforming humanity from within and making it new. The church evangelizes when She seeks to convert (Rom. 1:16), solely through the divine power of the Message She proclaims, both the personal and collective consciences of people, as well as the activities in which they engage, their lives and concrete surroundings.

19.   The Church seeks to upset humanity's criteria of judgment, prevailing values, points of interest, lines of thought, sources of inspiration and models in life which are in contrast with the Word of God and the plan of salvation.

20.   With the human person as the starting point and always coming back to the relationships of people among themselves and with God, every effort must be made to ensure the full evangelization of culture, or more correctly, of cultures. They have to be regenerated by an encounter with the Gospel. But this encounter will not take place if the Gospel is not proclaimed.

21.   Above all, the Gospel must be proclaimed by the witness of a Christian life. Such a witness is a silent proclamation of the Good News, very powerful and very effective. All Christians are called to this witness, and in this way they can be real evangelizers.

22.   Sooner or later, however, the Good News proclaimed by the living witness of a good life, has to be proclaimed by the word of life. There is no true evangelization if the name, the teaching, the life, the promises, the Kingdom and the mystery of Jesus of Nazareth, the Son of God, are not proclaimed.

23.   This proclamation reaches full development when it is listened to, accepted and assimilated, and when it evokes a genuine commitment in the one who has received it. Those whose lives have been transformed enter a community which is itself a sign of transformation, a sign of newness of life: it is the Church, the visible sacrament of Salvation.

24.   The person evangelized goes on to evangelize others. Herein lies the test of truth, the touchstone of evangelization.

Evangelization, therefore, is a complex process made up of varied elements: the renewal of humanity, witness, explicit proclamation, inner adherence, entry into the community, acceptance of signs, and apostolic initiative.

Chapter Three   THE CONTENT OF EVANGELIZATION

25.   The essential content, the living substance of the Church cannot be changed. The presentation, however, of secondary elements, of accidentals, depends greatly on changing circumstances.

26.   To evangelize is first of all to bear witness, in a simple and direct way, to God revealed by Jesus Christ, in the Holy Spirit; to bear witness that in His Son God has loved the world – that in His Incarnate Word He has given being to all things and has called every man and woman to eternal life.

27.   The center of the message is this: salvation in Jesus Christ. It is the clear proclamation that in Jesus Christ, the Son of God made man, salvation is offered to every human being. This is not an imminent salvation, meeting material or even spiritual needs, restricted to temporal existence and identified with temporal desires, hopes and struggles. It is a transcendent salvation which has its beginning in this life but which is fulfilled in eternity.

28.   Evangelization includes the prophetic proclamation of a hereafter, the preaching of hope in the promises made by God, the love of God and His love for us, the love of neighbor, the mystery of evil and the search for good, the search for God through prayer and the Sacraments. In its totality, evangelization consists in upholding and establishing the Church, which does not exist without the driving force which is the sacramental life culminating in the Eucharist.

29.   Evangelization, however, would not be complete if it did not take into account the rights and duties of every human being, of family life, life in society, peace, justice and development.

30.   The message of liberation from famine, chronic disease, illiteracy, poverty, injustices in international relations and commerce, situations of economic and cultural neo-colonialism, is not foreign to evangelization.

31.   Between evangelization and human advancement – development and liberation – there are profound anthropological and theological links. One cannot proclaim the new commandment without promoting the authentic advancement of humankind.

32.   Some good Christians in their wish to commit the Church to the liberation effort are frequently tempted to reduce her mission to a temporal project. They would reduced her aims to a human-centered goal, to material well-being. We wish to restate clearly the specifically religious finality of evangelization.

33.   Evangelization cannot be contained in the simple and restricted dimension of economics, politics, social or cultural life. It must take the whole person into account, in all aspects, right up to and including human openness to the absolute, even the divine Absolute.

34.   When preaching liberation, however, the Church is not willing to restrict her mission to the religious field and disassociate herself from temporal problems. Nevertheless she reaffirms the primacy of her spiritual vocation. Her contribution to liberation is incomplete if she neglects to proclaim salvation in Jesus Christ.

35.   Whenever its profound motives are not those of justice in charity, whenever its zeal lacks a truly spiritual dimension, and whenever its final goal is not salvation and happiness in God, all temporal liberation carries within itself the seeds of its own destruction.

36.   The best structures and the most idealized systems soon become inhuman if the inhuman inclinations of the human heart are not restrained.

37.   The Church cannot accept violence, especially in the force of arms – which is uncontrollable once it is let loose – and death as the path to liberation. Physical violence is not in accord with the Gospel. It is not Christian.

38.   Having said this, the Church is becoming ever more conscious of the proper manner and the evangelical means she possesses in order to collaborate in the liberation of people. She is trying more and more to encourage large numbers of Christians to devote themselves to the liberation of human beings.

39.   The necessity of ensuring fundamental human rights cannot be separated from liberation. Among these fundamental human rights, religious liberty occupies a primary place of importance.

Chapter Four   THE METHODS OF EVANGELIZATION

40.   The question of 'how to evangelize' is permanently relevant, because the methods of evangelizing vary according to the differing circumstances of time, place, and culture.

41.   Modern people listen more willingly to witnesses than to teachers, and when they do listen to teachers, it is because they are

witnesses. It is therefore primarily by her conduct, by her living witness of fidelity to the Lord Jesus, that the Church will evangelize the world.

42. The importance and necessity of preaching must be emphasized. "And how are they to believe in him of whom they have never heard? And how are they to hear without a preacher? ...So faith comes from what is heard and what is heard comes by the preaching of Christ" (Rom. 10:14 ff).

43. The homily is a very adaptable instrument of evangelization. Preaching has a particular role in evangelization, to the extent that it expresses the profound faith of the sacred minister and is impregnated with love.

44. In the effort to form patterns of Christian living that are more than notional, catechetical instruction of children and adolescents must not be neglected. Present conditions, moreover, render ever more urgent catechetical instructions, under the form of the catechumenate, for adults who, touched by grace, discover little by little the face of Christ and feel the need of giving themselves to him.

45. Mass media, put at the service of the Gospel, are capable of increasing almost indefinitely the area in which the Word of God is heard. The Church will feel guilty before the Lord if she does not utilize these powerful means.

46. Side-by-side with the collective proclamation of the Gospel, the person-to-person sharing of the Gospel is important. In the long run, is there any other way of handing on the Gospel than by sharing with another the personal experience of Faith? Through personal contact the conscience of the individual is reached and touched.

47. Yet, evangelization does not consist only of the preaching and teaching of doctrine. Evangelization exercises its full capacity when it achieves a permanent and unbroken intercommunication between Word and Sacrament. The role of evangelization is to educate people in the faith in such a way as to lead each individual Christian to live the sacraments as true sacraments of faith.

48. While popular piety has its limits, if it is well oriented, it is rich in values. It manifests a thirst for God which the simple and poor can know, involving an acute awareness of the fatherhood, the providence, the loving and constant presence of God. It makes people capable of generosity and sacrifice even to the point of heroism. It engenders patience, the sense of the Cross in daily life, detachment, openness to others, and devotion.

Chapter Five **THE BENEFICIARIES OF EVANGELIZATION**

49. "Go out to the whole world; proclaim the Good News to all creation" (Mk. 16:15) is addressed to everyone. The Twelve apostles and the first generation of Christians understood well the lesson of this text and similar ones. They made them into a program of action.

50. In the course of twenty centuries, the faithful have been tempted to narrow down the field of missionary activity. Do not imprison the proclamation of the Gospel by limiting it to one sector of humankind or to one class of people or to a single type of civilization. The Lord said: To the whole world! To all creation! To the ends of the earth!

51. To reveal Jesus Christ and his Gospel to those who do not know them has been the fundamental program which the Church received from her Founder. She carries this out by a complex and diversified program which is sometimes termed "pre-evangelization," but which is already evangelization in the true sense.

52. While the first proclamation is addressed especially to those who have never heard the Good News of Jesus, it also is necessary for innumerable people who have been baptized but who live outside Christian life.

53. The Church respects and esteems non-Christian religions because they are the living expression of the soul of vast groups of people. They possess an impressive religious patrimony. We wish to point out, however, that neither respect and esteem for these religions, nor the complexity of the questions raised, is an invitation to the Church to withhold from these non-Christians the proclamation of Jesus Christ. Our religion effectively establishes with God an authentic and living relationship which the other religions do not succeed in doing.

54. Unflagging attention is to be paid to those who have received the faith and who have been in contact with the Gospel for generations. The Church seeks to deepen, consolidate, nourish and make ever more mature the faith of those who are already called faithful or believers in order that they may further advance in the Christian life.

The Church also has a lively solicitude for the Christians who are not in full communion with her. While preparing with them the unity willed by Christ, she would be gravely lacking if she did not give witness before them of the fullness of the revelation whose deposit she guards.

55. Secularism is a phenomenon which is becoming a striking characteristic of the contemporary world: a concept of the world without any need for recourse to God. New forms of atheism seem to flow from it, a human-centered atheism, no longer abstract, but pragmatic, systematic and militant. Atheistic secularism can be seen in the consumer society, the pursuit of pleasure set up as the supreme value, the desire for power and domination, and in discrimination of every kind. This "humanism" generates inhuman tendencies.

56. The number of baptized who, for the most part, have not formally renounced their Baptism but who are indifferent to it and not living in accordance with it, is very large. The resistance of this group to evangelization takes the form of inertia and the slightly hostile attitude of the person who feels that he is one of the family, who claims to know and to have tried it all, and who no longer believes.

57. The Church sees before her an immense multitude of people who need the Gospel and have a right to it, for God "wants everyone to be saved and reach full knowledge of the truth" (I Tim. 2:4).

58. "Small communities" flourish more or less throughout the Church. They differ greatly among themselves: some in harmony with the Church, others in a spirit of bitter criticism of the Church. As hearers of the Gospel, the "small communities" in solidarity with the Church, soon become proclaimers of the Gospel themselves.

Chapter Six **WORKERS FOR EVANGELIZATION**

59. Who has the mission of evangelizing? By divine mandate, the duty of going out into the whole world and preaching the Gospel to every creature rests upon the whole Church. The work of evangelization is a basic duty of the People of God.

60. Evangelization is for no one an individual and isolated act. It is one that is deeply ecclesial. No evangelizer has sovereign control of the evangelizing action. All must act in communion with the Church and her pastors.

61. The first Christians readily expressed their deep faith in the Church by describing her as being spread throughout the world.

62. This universal Church, however, is alive in the individual Churches. The Church is universal by vocation and mission, but when she puts down Her roots in a variety of cultural, social and human situations, She takes on different external expressions and appearances in each part of the world.

63.   The individual Churches have the task of assimilating the essence of the Gospel message and of transposing it, without betrayal of its essential truth, into the language particular people understand, and then of proclaiming it in this language.

64.   Individual Churches should keep a profound openness toward the universal Church. Whenever an individual Church has cut itself off from the universal Church, it faces two equally serious dangers. The first danger is that of a withering isolationism. The second danger is that of losing its freedom when it finds itself alone and a prey to the most varied forces of suppression and exploitation.

65.   While translating the content of the Catholic faith into all expressions, this content must be neither impaired nor mutilated.

66.   In evangelization, the diversity of services in the unity of the same mission makes for richness and beauty.

67.   Christ's mandate to preach the Gospel pertains primarily and immediately to the Bishops with and under Peter.

68.   In union with the successor of Peter, the Bishops receive the authority to teach the revealed truth in the Church. Associated with the Bishops in the ministry of evangelization are those, who through priestly ordination, act in the person of Christ.

69.   Religious find in their consecrated lives a privileged means of effective evangelization. By their lives they are a sign of total availability to God, the Church, and the community.

70.   The laity, whose particular vocation places them in the midst of the world, must exercise a very special form of evangelization. Their task is to put to use every Christian and evangelical possibility latent in the affairs of the world.

71.   The family well deserves the beautiful name of "domestic Church." The family, like the Church, ought to be a place where the Gospel is transmitted, and from which the Gospel radiates. In a family which is conscious of this mission, all the members evangelize and are evangelized.

72.   Young people trained in faith and prayer must become more and more the apostles of youth. The Church counts greatly on their contribution.

73.   Seeking suitable ways of proclaiming the Gospel effectively, the laity exercise a great variety of ministries according to the grace and

charism which the Lord gives them. Special esteem is due to those lay people who consecrate a part of their time, their energies, and sometimes their entire lives, to the service of the missions.

Chapter Seven THE SPIRIT OF EVANGELIZATION

74. Evangelizers, be worthy of your vocation. Exercise it without doubt or fear. Do not neglect the conditions that will make your vocation active and fruitful.

75. The Holy Spirit is the principal agent of evangelization. It is He who inspires each individual to proclaim the Gospel, and it is He who causes the word of salvation to be understood and accepted. It was not by chance that the inauguration of evangelization took place on the morning of Pentecost, under the inspiration of the Spirit.

76. This century thirsts for authenticity. Do you really believe what you are proclaiming? Do you live what you believe? Do you preach what you live? The world expects from us simplicity of life, the spirit of prayer, obedience, humility, detachment and self-sacrifice.

77. Divisions among Christians seriously impede the work of Christ. This is one of the great obstacles to evangelization today. We desire collaboration with other Christian communities with whom we are not yet united in perfect unity. We take as a basis for this collaboration the foundation of Baptism and the patrimony of the faith which is common to us. The duty of giving witness to the Gospel requires this.

78. Every evangelizer is expected to reverence the truth. Our pastoral service impels us to preserve, defend, and to communicate the truth regardless of the sacrifices that this involves.

79. The work of evangelization presupposes in the evangelizer an ever increasing love for those whom one is evangelizing.

80. Lack of fervor is a great obstacle to evangelization. It is manifested in fatigue, disenchantment, compromise, lack of interest, and above all, lack of joy and hope. It is true that human beings by God's mercy can gain salvation even though the Gospel is not preached to them. But, as for us, can we gain salvation if through negligence or fear or shame or the result of false ideas we fail to preach the Gospel?

CONCLUSION

81.   These years mark the eve of a new century, the eve of the third millennium of Christianity. With evangelization as its basic feature, may the light of Christ shine through a program of pastoral action.

82.   On the morning of Pentecost the Immaculate Blessed Virgin Mary watched over the beginnings of evangelization prompted by the Holy Spirit. May she be the star of evangelization in these times which are both difficult and full of hope.

Pope John Paul II's Gift

(December 7, 1990)

INTRODUCTION

1.   The mission of Christ the Redeemer, entrusted to the Church, is far from completion; it is still only beginning. The Spirit impels us, like Paul (I Cor. 9:16), to focus on the *urgency of missionary activity*. Basing the Church's "missionary nature" on the Trinity, the Second Vatican Council sought to renew the entire Church in light of the needs of the contemporary world (Jn. 17:21).

2.   Among the many fruits of the Council, a new awareness has grown: *missionary activity is a matter for all Christians*. However, some difficulties exist and missionary activity *ad gentes* (specifically directed "to the nations") appears to be waning. Is this a crisis of faith?

Thus, in continuity with *Ad Gentes* (1965) and *Evangelii Nuntiandi* (1975), this encyclical invites the Church to *renew her missionary commitment* because *faith is strengthened when it is given to others*. Missionary evangelization is the primary service the Church can render

---

Caution: This is an unofficial summary of a lengthy papal document. It is provided to popularize and disseminate the important ideas of this mission encyclical. Although care has been taken to provide a "faithful summary," any formal discussion of mission and evangelization should use the complete official text.

to modern humanity. All mission has but one purpose: to serve people by revealing God's love made manifest in Jesus Christ.

3.   In full respect for every people, culture, and religion, the Pope extends the invitation: *Peoples everywhere, open the doors to Christ*. In our times momentous changes continue to unfold; these provide God-given opportunities for the Church to sow the Gospel and promote a new evangelization, to proclaim Christ to all peoples.

Chapter One   JESUS CHRIST, THE ONLY SAVIOR

4.   The Church's fundamental and continuous function is to direct all humanity toward the mystery of Christ. This task is born of faith in Jesus Christ. In fact, it is only in faith that the Church's entire mission is adequately understood. Faith will be central in answering many aspects of the questions: *Why should there be missionary activity? Is missionary work among non-Christians still relevant?*

5.   The early Church as well as the entire New Testament affirm the universality of salvation in Christ (Acts 4:10, 12; I Cor. 8:5-6; Jn. 1:9, 18; 14:6). In Jesus, God's revelation becomes definitive and complete (Heb. 1:1-2; 4:14-16; I Tim. 2:5-7). This revelation of *who he is* places Jesus at the foundation of the Church's missionary identity. Therefore, other participated forms of mediation acquire meaning and value *only* from Christ's own mediation; they cannot be understood as parallel or complementary to Jesus Christ's mediation.

6.   It is contrary to Christian faith to separate Jesus from the Christ, to detach a "Jesus of history" from the "Christ of faith." This uniqueness of Christ is abundantly clear from Scripture (Jn. 1:2, 14, 16, 18; Mt. 16:16; Col. 1:13-14, 19-20; 2:9; Rev. 22:13); he has an absolute and universal significance. Christians legitimately explore the various aspects of the rich mystery of Christ, the one center of God's unified plan of salvation (Eph. 1:10).

Christological faith also demands that "we are obliged to hold that the Holy Spirit offers everyone the possibility of sharing in the Paschal Mystery in a manner known to God" (GS 22); [note that this quote is used verbatim three times in the encyclical: RM 6, 10, 28].

7.   The urgency of missionary activity derives from the *radical newness of life* brought by Christ. God lovingly offers humanity this gift of new life; it is freely given. It is also accepted or rejected through one's

human freedom. Faith in Christ is always directed to humanity's authentic freedom.

8.   Any true vision of humanity cannot focus on the horizontal dimension alone – without an openness to the Absolute. The Second Vatican Council promoted an authentic "new humanity" which includes safeguarding freedom of conscience. Thus the Church's mission of proclaiming Christ and bearing witness to him, when done in a way that respects consciences, does not violate freedom. In fact, human dignity is promoted through proclaiming the riches of the mystery of Christ.

9.   Christ dwells within the Church and carries out his mission through her. The Church is both sign and instrument of salvation; she believes that God established Christ as the one mediator and that she herself is the universal sacrament of salvation. To understand the *one mystery of salvation*, it is necessary to keep two core truths together, namely, the real possibility of salvation in Christ for all humanity and the necessity of the Church for salvation. Or again, salvation remains the Holy Spirit's gift but requires human cooperation.

10.   Grace and salvation are universally offered to all people. Whether formally part of the Church or not, all have a relationship to the Church by Christ's grace and the Holy Spirit's action. The centrality of the Paschal Mystery is operative universally; thus, (for the second time in the encyclical) it is asserted that "we are obliged to hold that the Holy Spirit offers everyone the possibility of sharing in this Paschal Mystery in a manner known to God" (cf. RM 6, 28).

11.   In response to objections regarding mission *ad gentes*, Christians continually reaffirm their faith in Christ; in this they imitate Paul (Rom. 1:16) and the Christian martyrs of all times. Convinced that the Gospel always remains "Good News," they believe that true liberation consists in opening oneself to Christ's love and peace (II Cor. 5:14; Eph. 2:14).

Many answers can be given to the question: *"Why mission"?* Fundamentally, *mission is an issue of faith*, an accurate indicator of our faith in Christ and his love for us. In affirming that Jesus came to bring integral salvation, the Church-in-mission heralds the "unsearchable riches of Christ" (Eph. 3:8). She remains faithful to the Lord's mandate and the presence of God's life within her. It is her privilege to continue *bearing witness to the faith and to the Christian life* – all as sincere service to peoples everywhere.

Chapter Two   THE KINGDOM OF GOD

12.   Christ is the incarnate revelation of God who is "rich in mercy." The Father's love is freely given in Jesus through the Spirit – thus, God's kingdom is unfolded. The kingdom, prepared for in the Old Testament, is inaugurated by and in Christ, proclaimed to all peoples by the Church as she works and prays for its full realization. God's kingdom action in the Old Testament is accomplished through his chosen people (Gen. 9:1-17; 12:3; Dt. 4:37; 7:6-8; Is. 2:2-5; 25:6-8; 43:1-7; 60:1-6; Jer. 3:17; 16:19).

13.   Jesus of Nazareth, the fulfillment of God's plan, had as his mission the proclamation and establishment of the kingdom. All the evangelists illustrate how Jesus in his person makes the kingdom present: Mark (1:14-15; 3:13-19; 14:36), Matthew (4:17; 6:10; 7:21; 11:4-5; 12:25-28; 20:1-6; 23:9), Luke (4:14-21, 43; 11:2; 15:3-32), John (I Jn. 4:8, 16). Jesus is the kingdom in person; the "Good News" is Christ!

14.   Through his words, his actions, and his own person, Jesus gradually reveals the characteristics and demands of the kingdom (Lk. 4:18; 5:24, 30; 6:20; 7:34; 15:1-32; 18:42-43; Mt. 12:28). Two special gestures are characteristic of Jesus' mission: healing and forgiving; through these and other signs Jesus manifested the emergence of God's reign.

15.   The kingdom seeks transformed human values and relationships based on love, service, and forgiveness. The law of love must dominate all relations – with one another and with God (Mt. 22:34-40; Lk. 10:25-28; Jn. 3:16; 13:34; 15:12-13). Working for the kingdom means acknowledging and promoting God's activity and plan of salvation in all its fullness.

16.   In the risen Christ God's kingdom is fulfilled and proclaimed, giving a universal scope to Jesus' message, his actions and whole mission (Mt. 28:18; Acts 2:36; Eph. 1:18-21). The disciples continue preaching Jesus Christ risen, with whom the kingdom is identified (Acts 8:12; 28:31; Eph. 5:5; II Pt. 1:11; Rev. 11:15; 12:10). The Church today necessarily unites *the proclamation of the kingdom of God* (the content of Jesus' own kerygma) and *the proclamation of the Christ-event* (the kerygma of the apostles); these two proclamations are complementary.

17.   Any presentation of the kingdom must be consonant with the Church's thinking; reductive views that are secularized and closed to the transcendent easily become an ideology of purely earthly progress.

The promotion of "kingdom values" and dialogue between peoples, cultures, and religions can truly be positive if they incorporate Christ and the mystery of redemption in its fullness. God's kingdom is not limited to this world (Jn. 18:36).

18.   The kingdom of God simply cannot be detached either from Christ or from the Church. Jesus is the kingdom in person and its final goal (Mk. 10:45; I Cor. 15:27); before all else the kingdom is *a person* with the face and name of Jesus of Nazareth. Likewise, the Church is intimately ordered toward the kingdom of God of which she is the seed, sign, and instrument.

19.   The foregoing comprehensive perspective is necessary for understanding the reality of the kingdom. It prevents one from falling into any form of "ecclesiocentrism." Following the lead of Paul VI, the church continually explores the profound links between Christ, the Church and evangelization.

20.   Concrete and effective service of the kingdom remains the Church's task. She calls people to conversion (Jn. 1:12), establishes faith communities, promotes "gospel values" in the world, and opens peoples' horizons to the works of the Spirit (Jn. 3:8).

These tasks seek to strengthen the foundations and purposes of missionary activity. As a dynamic force in humanity's journey, the church becomes the sacrament of salvation for all humankind. She never compromises her eschatological vision and awaits the time when Christ "delivers the kingdom to God the Father" and "God will be everything to everyone" (I Cor. 15:24, 28).

Chapter Three   **THE HOLY SPIRIT: THE PRINCIPAL AGENT OF MISSION**

21.   John Paul II wrote in his encyclical on the Holy Spirit (DV 42) that "At the climax of Jesus' messianic mission, the Holy Spirit becomes present in the Paschal Mystery in all of his divine subjectivity." Thus, the Spirit now continues the salvific work of Jesus' sacrifice on the cross. True, Jesus missions the apostles and the Church, but the Holy Spirit remains the principal agent of the whole of the Church's mission. The Spirit's preeminent action is clearly seen in the early Church (Acts 10; 15; 16:6 ff.).

22. All four Evangelists record resurrection encounters between the risen Christ and the apostles and conclude their narratives with the "missionary mandate" (Mt. 28:18-20; Mk. 16:15-18; Lk. 24:46-49; Jn. 20:21-23). Christ, who was sent by the Father, sends his own into the world in the power of the Spirit. All mission becomes *a sending forth in the Spirit.*

23. Two common elements found in all versions of the "missionary mandate" are the universalism of the mission task (Mk. 16:15; Mt. 28:19; Lk. 24:47; Acts 1:8) and the assurance of the Lord's continual presence (Mk. 16:20; Mt. 28:20). The unique or particular emphases found are the following: Mark presents mission as proclamation or kerygma (8:29; 15:39; 16:15); Matthew has an ecclesiological emphasis (16:18; 28:19-20); Luke sees mission as witness (24:48; Acts 1:8, 22); John emphasizes the sending/mandate aspect of mission (17:3, 18, 21-23; 20:21). Mission admits of pluralism (in charisms, circumstances, and peoples) within the overall unified task.

At its core, the mission of the disciples always emanates from Christ's mission. Not based on human abilities, mission relies on the power of the risen Lord. We are first missionaries because of *what we are* (in Christ's love) even before becoming missionaries *in word or deed.*

24. The mission of Jesus and the Church is the work of God and the Spirit. Pentecost transformed Jesus' followers into *witnesses and prophets* (Acts 1:8; 2:17-18), empowered with serene courage and "boldness" to go to the ends of the earth.

Six model "missionary discourses" are recorded in Acts (2:22-39; 3:12-26; 4:9-12; 5:29-32; 10:34-43; 13:16-41). The Spirit also moves mission to the Gentiles (Acts 13:46-48) and guides the first Church Council (Acts 15:5-11, 28).

25. The evangelization of the Gentiles demands "dialogue" with peoples' hopes and expectations, their anguish and sufferings, their cultural and religious values (Acts 14:15-17; 17:18, 22-31). This process unfolds examples of the inculturation of the Gospel. It is always the spirit who directs this truly universal mission.

26. The Spirit's action enabled the early Christian community to live in "fraternal communion" *(koinonia)* and to be of one heart and soul (Acts 2:42-47; 4:32-35). The example and life-style of the community in Acts verify the truth that even before activity, mission means witness and a way of life that shines out to others.

27. The whole Church, which is missionary by the Spirit's action, moves into mission on many levels. Mission, first directed to Israel, expands to the Gentiles. Mission is lived by Peter and the Twelve, by the community of believers (Acts 2:46-47), and by special envoys (Acts 13:1-4). Mission as a community commitment and responsibility of the local Church is presented by Luke in Acts as the normal outcome of Christian living.

28. The Spirit's special manifestation in the Church and her members does not exclude or limit the active presence of the Spirit in every time and place. As noted by the Vatican Council, the Spirit works in everyone's heart through the "seeds of the Word" found in human initiatives – including religious ones. Once again it is said: "we are obliged to hold that the Holy Spirit offers everyone the possibility of sharing in the Paschal Mystery in a manner known to God" (cf. RM 6, 10). The Spirit's presence and activity affect not only individuals but also society and history, peoples, cultures and religions.

29. The wide expanse of the Spirit's activity (Wis. 1:7; Jn. 3:8; 16:13) necessarily guides interaction with all peoples; the interreligious meeting in Assisi manifested this fact. In approaching the followers of other religions, the Church always respects the person as well as the action of the Spirit in each person. Two principles apply: the work of the Spirit is harmoniously linked to Jesus the Christ; the universal activity of the Spirit is never separated from his particular activity within Christ's body, the Church. The same Spirit is at work; his presence must continually be discerned by the Church.

30. As seen in humanity's history, contemporary events are major turning points and demand *a resurgence of the Church's missionary activity.* In our own time new horizons are opening; missionary activity is only beginning. Today all Christians, the particular Churches and the universal Church, are called to listen to the Spirit's voice; *he is the principal agent of mission!*

Chapter Four   **THE VAST HORIZONS OF THE MISSION
AD GENTES**

31. In the apostles, the Church received a universal mission – to bring fullness of life and God's love to all nations (Jn. 10:10). This mission is one and undivided, although within it there are different tasks and activities. Never can the church withdraw from her *permanent mission of bringing the Gospel* to the multitudes, her *mission ad gentes.*

32.   When considering today's complex and ever-changing religious picture, one observes phenomena such as urbanization, migration, refugees, de-christianization, the proliferation of messianic cults and religious sects. These difficult challenges are to be balanced by noting the fruits of mission work, particularly the well-established young Churches. Should the "language of mission" be modified to speak of a *single missionary situation*? Is it still appropriate to focus on *specific missionary activity?*

Raising these questions has had positive results: *missiology* has been inserted into ecclesiology; the Trinitarian emphasis within mission has provided fresh enthusiasm. Yet, distinctions remain important. Affirming the missionary nature of the whole Church does not preclude either the existence of a specific mission *ad gentes* or the requirement for the specific vocation of life-long missionaries *ad gentes.*

33.   The diversity of activities *in the Church's one mission* is factually clear. From the viewpoint of evangelization, *three situations* can be identified: (1) situations in which Christ and his Gospel are not known (here mission *ad gentes* applies – in the proper sense of the term); (2) contexts where there are healthy Christian communities (they require pastoral care); (3) areas where many baptized have lost a living faith-sense (here a "new evangelization" or "re-evangelization" is needed).

34.   While the boundaries between *pastoral care of the faithful, new evangelization,* and *specific missionary activity* are not clearly definable, there should be no lessening of the impetus for mission *ad gentes* to the "non-Christians." Certainly, mission ad gentes retains its value; it gives essential meaning to the Church's missionary identity.

A growing *interdependence* among the three situations of evangelization is noted today. Ideally, the result should be that missionary activity *ad intra* (inwardly) becomes a credible, stimulating sign for missionary activity *ad extra* (outwardly), and vice versa.

35.   The Church's mission *ad gentes* faces a great challenge: to go to all peoples even in spite of difficulties. The task seems disproportional to the Church's human resources. However, mission is not a merely human enterprise. Thus, faith-filled missionaries confidently approach such *difficulties* as refusal of entry, laws forbidding evangeli-

zation and worship, presumed irrelevance of the Gospel, and the misinterpretation of conversion.

36. As Pope Paul VI noted, *difficulties* also exist *within* the People of God. The most serious of these is "a widespread indifferentism" which is characterized by "a religious relativism." Some even try to claim support for such attitudes in the teaching of the Council. Renewed "thinking with the Church" *(sentire cum Ecclesia)* is needed. Pessimism should be avoided because of our faith in Jesus Christ and his Spirit as the principal agents of the Church's mission. We are enthusiastic co-workers and servants – doing our missionary duty (Lk. 17:10).

37. While asserting that mission *ad gentes* is universal and knows no boundaries, it is important to discuss various parameters of the Church's mission activity.

(a) *Territorial Limits.* The criterion of geography, while not totally precise, helps focus the task of mission within vast regions still to be evangelized – particularly in Asia, but also in Africa, Latin America, and Oceania.

(b) *New Worlds and New Social Phenomena.* Today's rapid and profound transformations in the world (especially urbanization in massive cities) demand a re-imaging of mission *ad gentes.* While not neglecting small groups of people, mission efforts need to be concentrated on the big cities where the future of younger nations is being shaped. These cities are home to many youth, migrants, refugees and poverty is often rampant.

(c) *Cultural sectors: the modern equivalents of the Areopagus.* Paul's preaching of the Gospel in the Areopagus of Athens (Acts 17:22-31) has its contemporary parallels; examples are: the *world of communications,* mass media, peace and development movements, human rights (especially for minorities, women, and children), ecology, scientific research and international relations. In all these fields, mission seeks to bridge the split between Gospel and culture.

38. Our momentous times contain many ambiguities: consumerism and materialism on one side with a search for meaning and the need of an inner life on the other. This phenomenon (the so-called "religious revival") represents an opportunity for the Church to announce Christ as "the way, the truth, and the life" (Jn. 14:6).

39. All forms of mission must faithfully follow Christ – in both death and resurrection. And, the Church insists on her right to proclaim Christ and God's plan in an atmosphere of religious freedom. Proclamation and mission respect human rights and freedom; *the Church proposes; she imposes nothing.* To all peoples the Church repeats: *Open the doors to Christ!* Openness is also demanded of all particular Churches – an openness to missionaries, an openness which overcomes cultural and nationalistic barriers and avoids isolationism.

40. Even as the end of the second millennium of the redemption approaches, missionary activity still represents the greatest challenge for the Church. In fact, mission *ad gentes* is still in its infancy and directs our attention toward the South and the East. Apostolic concern and enthusiastic outreach always remain an integral dimension of every Christian's faith.

Chapter Five   THE PATHS OF MISSION

41. Missionary activity is centered on manifesting God's salvific plan and its fulfillment in the world and in history. Mission is a single but complex reality, and it develops in a variety of ways.

42. Following the model of Christ, the "witness" *par excellence* (Rev. 1:5; 3;14), Christian living and concern is the first form of all mission, a form particularly appealing to people today. *The very life of the missionary, of the Christian family,* and *of the ecclesial community* must reveal a new way of living. This evangelical witness (sometimes the only possible way of being a missionary) takes many forms but its concern is always for people and is directed toward integral human development.

43. Christians are called to be signs of the integration of the Gospel with their native land, people and national culture, while remaining open to universal brotherhood. Their witnessing to Christ calls them to courageous and prophetic stands in the face of corruption and to use resources to humbly serve the poorest of the poor.

44. Explicit Gospel proclamation remains the permanent priority of mission; it always contains as its foundation, center, and summit a clear focus on universal salvation in Jesus Christ (Eph. 3:3-9; Col. 1:25-29). Though mission is a complex reality, all its forms are directed to this proclamation of "Good News" – Christ crucified and risen. In this proclamation the Spirit is at work. Missioners strive to contextualize this Gospel message within people's lives and daily situations.

45. Proclamation, never a merely personal act, is profoundly linked to the evangelizing activity of the whole Church. It is necessarily faith-inspired and results in enthusiasm, courage *(parrhesia)*, and fervor (I Th. 2:2; Eph. 6:18-20).

In their proclamation missionaries acknowledge the pre-existing action of the Spirit – raising people's expectation and openness to God's truth. The Spirit of the Father speaks through evangelizers (Mt. 10:17-20; Lk. 12:11-12; Acts 5:32; Rom. 1:16). The martyrs of history and of today are *par excellence* the heralds and witnesses of the faith.

46. The proclamation of the Word of God has *Christian conversion* as its aim. Conversion is a gift and work of the Trinity (Jn. 6:44; I Cor. 12:3). It is total and radical, a dynamic and lifelong process; it means living in the Spirit (Rom. 8:3-13) and accepting, by a personal decision, the saving sovereignty of Christ.

The Church calls people to conversion, as did John the Baptist (Mk. 1:4) and Jesus himself (Mk. 1:14-15); *repent* and believe in the Gospel. Though questions are raised about conversion, the Church affirms the right of everyone to hear and respond to the "Good News" as did the Samaritan woman (Jn. 4:10, 15).

47. Peter and the apostles, prompted by the Spirit, preached conversion and baptism (Acts 2:37-38; 3:19). Baptism and conversion are intimately linked in the Church's practice by the will of Christ himself (Mt. 28:19) and by intrinsic need (Jn. 3: 5). Conversion to Christ cannot be separated from Baptism; Baptism remains necessary. Thus, local ecclesial communities must devote themselves to this double task, remembering that each baptized convert is a special gift to the Church. We, as Christians, frequently recall that we cannot preach conversion unless we ourselves are converted anew every day.

48. Because conversion and baptism give entry into the Church community, mission *ad gentes* seeks to found and develop Christian communities. When these local communities are mature, the whole mystery of the Church is contained in each particular Church (cf. AG 19-22). These Churches, in turn, also become missionary.

49. The establishment of Christian communities everywhere *(plantatio Ecclesiae)* still remains an unfinished task – the responsibility of every Church, missionary by its nature as well as both evangelized and evangelizing. To be a Church-in-mission requires radical conver-

sion; it is also the clearest sign of a mature faith. Missionary personnel, working in communion with their local counterparts, actively encourage a dynamic missionary sense within the particular Churches, following the solicitude of Christ the Good Shepherd (Jn. 10:16).

50. In the process of forming local Churches, there should be emphasis on *missionary activity* and *ecumenical activity*. Division among Christians weakens their witness; reconciliation is needed to augment their communion which, though imperfect, does exist among the baptized. Ecumenical witness can address the confusion sown by Christian and para-Christian sects – a clear threat for the Church today.

51. The expanding phenomenon of "ecclesial basic communities" in many young Churches is a welcomed force for evangelization. These local groups gather for prayer, Scripture reading, catechesis, and discussion on human and ecclesial problems; they become a true leaven in Christian life; within them individuals experience Christian community (Acts 2:42-47). As they function in communion with their pastors, they are cause for great hope in Church life.

52. The need to incarnate the Gospel in peoples' culture is particularly urgent today. Inculturation signifies "the intimate transformation of authentic cultural values through their integration in Christianity and the insertion of Christianity in the various human cultures." Through this lengthy and profound process both the Church and the Christian message are mutually enriched. Inculturation enables the Church to be a more effective instrument of mission and to better express the mystery of Christ.

53. Missionaries immerse themselves in their new cultural milieu so as to better bring people the knowledge of God's mystery (Rom. 16:25-27; Eph. 3:5). The developing local ecclesial communities strive to translate the treasures of the faith into legitimate, inculturated expressions.

54. The inculturation process is guided by two principles: "compatibility with the Gospel and communion with the universal Church." Culture must be treasured but not overestimated; as a human creation, it needs to be "healed, ennobled and perfected." Inculturation allows the Christian "mystery" to grow within the genius of a people; it involves the whole people of God and maturely reflects their authentic *sensus fidei*.

55. Interreligious dialogue with our brothers and sisters of other religions is part of the Church's evangelizing mission; it is not in

opposition to mission *ad gentes*. The Council acknowledged God's presence to individuals and entire peoples through their spiritual riches, of which their religions are the main and essential expression. These assertions do not detract from the fact that *salvation comes from Christ and that dialogue does not dispense from evangelization.*

Proclaiming Christ and engaging in interreligious dialogue are not in conflict. The availability of God's grace and salvation to all does not negate *the need for the Church.* Thus, dialogue proceeds with the conviction that *the Church is the ordinary means of salvation* and that she alone possesses the fullness of the means of salvation.

56.   Dialogue is founded on deep respect, not tactical concerns or self-interest. It seeks to uncover the "seeds of the Word" and to bear fruit in the Spirit. All dialogue partners must be both consistent with their religious convictions and genuinely open to the other believers. True dialogue leads to inner transformation and is spiritually fruitful.

57.   The field of dialogue is vast with many forms and expressions. All Christians – especially the laity – are called to dialogue in their daily lives. Missionaries should persevere even when the difficult path of dialogue is their only avenue of bearing sincere witness to Christ. Dialogue will certainly be fruitful, even if the Father alone knows the times and seasons (Acts 1:7).

58.   Today mission *ad gentes* continues. Frequently missionaries are recognized as promoters of development and integral liberation. As noted in *Sollicitudo Rei Socialis,* the Church's contribution promotes development by forming people's consciences. In brief, "authentic human development must be rooted in an ever deeper evangelization." The Church's focus is always the person, not material or technological growth: *the human being is the principal agent of development.*

59.   Church involvement in development promotes human dignity and seeks a place for everyone in God's plan. Its foundation is the biblical perspective of the "new heavens and a new earth" (Is. 65:17; II Pt. 3:13; Rev. 21:1). It hopes to lead people to God and avoid "soulless development." It calls for conversion: "Fight hunger by changing your lifestyle." In short, such *missionary activity* seeks an "integral development" open to the Absolute.

60.   To be the Church of the poor and to live Christ's Beatitudes are the Church's sincere desire. Thus, in her mission the poor deserve preferential attention, and their evangelization is *par excellence* the sign and proof of the mission of Jesus. Disciples of Jesus need to

sincerely review their lives regarding their solidarity with the poor. Missionaries deserve gratitude for their work for the integral development of individuals and of society. The Church's many "works of charity" reveal that *love* remains the *driving force of mission*. Or again, charity is the source and criterion of all mission.

Chapter Six   **LEADERS AND WORKERS IN THE MISSIONARY APOSTOLATE**

61.   Without missionaries there is no mission activity. So Jesus chooses and sends his witnesses forth to the ends of the earth (Acts 1:8). The Twelve, the "collegial subject" of mission, go forth (Mt. 10:6); James, John and, above all, Peter are witnesses (Acts 2:14, 37); Paul's work extends to the nations (Gal. 1:15-16); the local Church at Antioch becomes an evangelizing community (Acts 13:2-3).

62.   The mission activity of the early Church retains all its validity and urgency today; *the Church is missionary by her very nature*. Young Churches – even with a clergy shortage – should begin sharing in the Church's universal missionary work. Younger and older Churches mutually need each others' strength, witness and riches.

63.   As the risen Lord missioned Peter and the College of the Apostoles, their successors have primary responsibility for missionary activity. Pope John Paul II views his travels as journeys of faith for proclaiming the Gospel. Bishops, collectively and individually, should pay special attention to missionary activity, the greatest and holiest duty of the Church.

64.   Bishops, Episcopal Conferences, and all particular Churches must be generous – even from their poverty and deficiencies – and send missionaries *ad gentes*. Following Church *norms* regarding clergy distribution, all Churches are invited to share the Pope's concern and promote missionary vocations.

65.   The mission decree *Ad Gentes* devoted a special chapter to "missionaries" and emphasize their fundamental importance and special task in evangelization. Missionaries and religious institutes keep mission *ad gentes* as their "special vocation"; their commitment involves their whole person and entire life.

66.   Missionary institutes, faithful to their founding charism, exist for the Church and cooperate with *Propaganda Fide* for the spread of the faith and the founding of new Churches. Such institutes remain "absolutely necessary." Likewise, the special vocation of missionaries *"for life"* retains all its validity; it is the model of the Church's missionary commitment.

67. All priests must have the mind and heart of missionaries – open to the needs of the Church and the world. *The true Catholic spirit* always promotes *the most universal and all embracing mission of salvation* that extends to earth's ends. Such a universal vision demands great maturity of priests in their vocation.

68. Pope Pius XII, with prophetic insight, encouraged diocesan priests (*"Fidei Donum* priests") to serve the universal mission of the Church. Such service, though temporary, is a valuable contribution to the growth of needy ecclesial communities.

69. Inspired by the Spirit, *Institutes of Consecrated Life* have borne much missionary fruitfulness and have rendered outstanding service. *Institutes of Contemplative Life*, through their presence in the young Churches, highlight the value of contemplation and asceticism. *Institutes of Active Life* do immense charity work, extend God's kingdom, and bear effective witness by their total self-gift in chastity, poverty, and obedience.

70. Missionary religious sisters deserve a special word of appreciation. Their "gift of self with love in a total and undivided manner" is an indispensable evangelical sign – particularly where women still have far to go on the way to full liberation.

71. Recent popes and their writings (e.g. *Christifideles Laici*) have stressed the responsibility and importance of the lay faithful in missionary activity. All the laity are missionaries by baptism and their participation in mission has been affirmed by the Second Vatican Council. The important contribution of women and the role of the laity in founding some Churches must not be overlooked. Laity's particular competence lies in seeking the kingdom of God by engaging in temporal affairs.

72. The sphere of lay presence and activity is very extensive. The recent growth of "ecclesial movements" is God's gift both for new evangelization and for missionary activity properly so-called. Those laity involved in mission *ad gentes* are cooperators with the local churches in the "planting of the Church" *(plantatio Ecclesiae)*.

73. Among the evangelizing ministries in the Church, catechists have a place of honor. Churches that are flourishing today owe much of

their progress to the ministry of catechists, who are specialists, direct witnesses, and irreplaceable evangelizers. The difficult ministry of catechist will always be necessary; their educational and personal needs should be properly addressed.

74.   Besides catechists, a wide variety of ministries serve the Church and her mission. All the laity are invited to devote some time to the Church as a sign of living their faith authentically.

75.   In an ecclesiology of communion in which the entire Church is missionary, coordination is necessary for fruitful mission activity. The competent Church body directing mission efforts is the Congregation for the Evangelization of Peoples. Unity which Christ prayed for (Jn. 17:21) should characterize the Mystical Body; all Dicasteries, Episcopal Conferences, major religious superiors and lay organizations should strive to coordinate their worldwide efforts for mission *ad gentes*.

76.   Episcopal Conferences help coordinate missionary activity and inculturation on national and regional levels and within other bodies of the same Conference; this effort avoids relegating mission concerns to one sector alone. Various missionary institutes should promote joint initiatives and cooperative structures for missionary activity.

Chapter Seven   COOPERATION IN MISSIONARY ACTIVITY

77.   As baptized Christians, all members of the Church share responsibility for mission; this community duty is termed "missionary cooperation." It is rooted in personal union with Christ (Jn. 15:5) and is manifested in holiness of life and mature faith. It flows over into prayer for the missions and missionary vocations as well as the assistance and welcome extended to missioners in imitation of the first Christian communities (Acts 14:27).

78.   The first form of missionary sharing is spiritual cooperation through prayer, sacrifice and Christian living. Prayer promotes effective proclamation. Sacrifice affirms the redemptive value of suffering in union with Christ (Col. 1:24). These truths enable the sick and suffering to become true missionaries. Pentecost – the beginning of the Church's mission – can be celebrated as a "Day of Suffering for the Missions."

79.   Promoting missionary vocations is a key form of cooperation in mission. The Church reaffirms that *a full and lifelong commitment*

to the work of the missions holds pride of place. The Gospel is preached above all by men and women who are consecrated for life to this work. This *concern for missionary vocations* requires analysis of vocation realities and prospects today: Where are the signs of the Church's vitality?

80.   Promoting mission vocations is a serious challenge, as Pope John Paul II has noted. He appeals to parents and families to foster vocations among their children. He asks youth to listen to Christ's call (Mt. 4:19) and to respond "Here I am, Lord! I am ready! Send me!" (cf. Is. 6:8). A life dedicated to proclaiming the "Good News" will be filled with genuine joy.

81.   Material and financial needs are many – especially in poor mission countries. Generous contributions and sacrifices that show love are genuinely appreciated. Our spirit of sharing should include both giving a contribution and participating in mission work itself. Inspired by faith, Christians realize that it is more blessed to give than to receive (Acts 20:35). *World Mission Day* teaches an important lesson: to make an offering to God, in the Eucharistic celebration and for all the missions of the world.

82.   The phenomenon of mobility has opened new forms of missionary cooperation. International tourism enables mutual cultural enrichment and direct exposure to missionary life – especially by the youth. There are opportunities to meet and bear witness to the followers of other religions – both abroad and at home; these are occasions to practice hospitality, dialogue, service, sharing, witness and direct proclamation. Increasing world interdependence affords additional opportunities for missionary cooperation.

83.   The promotion of missionary awareness and formation among the People of God is a central task of each local Church; it is a key element in the normal pastoral activity of parishes – especially among youth groups. Mission publications and audiovisual aids facilitate this awareness. Priestly formation should not ignore the Church's universal mission, ecumenism, the great religions and missiology. Such efforts seek to present an integral picture of mission which proclaims salvation in Christ and aims to satisfy the poor's hunger for God.

84.   The leading role in promoting a universal missionary spirit among the People of God belongs to the *Pontifical Mission Societies*; the Missionary Union fulfills the same task among all priests and religious. Their motto is: all the Churches united for the conversion of

the whole world. Thus, they foster worldwide, national, and local cooperation in harmony with the Congregation for the Evangelization of Peoples. The Pope also recommends they focus efforts on fostering lifelong vocations *ad gentes*.

85.   Mature missionary cooperation is open to mutuality, both giving and receiving benefits. In this spirit the Pope exhorts all the Churches: *be open to the Church's universality*. Temptations to provincialism, exclusiveness, and isolation can be strong. Older Churches may think their mission is now at home; younger Churches, concerned with their own inculturated identity, may close their doors to missionaries. All Churches must avoid isolationism and obey God's will (Acts 5:29).

86.   As the third millennium of the redemption approaches, we can see hopeful signs that God is preparing a new Springtime for the Gospel. People everywhere are refocusing on Gospel ideals and values (e.g. rejection of war, violence, racism; respect for human persons and women's dignity). We are sustained by Christian hope and prayer (Mt. 6:10). We are committed to a new missionary advent – a time for enthusiasm – an opportunity to announce the love of God in Jesus to waiting millions.

Chapter Eight   MISSIONARY SPIRITUALITY

87.   Being in mission demands a specific spirituality. It is complete docility to the lead of the Spirit that enables missionaries to bear witness to Christ with fortitude and discernment. By the Spirit's power the apostles were transformed into courageous witnesses and enlightened heralds. Like the first Christians, evangelizers today face challenges (Acts 4:26) and must allow themselves to be led by the Spirit (Jn. 16:13).

88.   The key to comprehending mission is linking it to Christ the one who was sent to evangelize. Mission spirituality, therefore, demands an intimate living of the Mystery of Christ. It is a path of total self-emptying (Phil. 2:5-8) and always leads to the foot of the cross. It demands poverty, brotherhood and solidarity (I Cor. 9:22-23), as well as confidence in the Lord's presence (Acts 18:9-10).

89.   Apostolic charity is another hallmark of mission spirituality. It reflects Christ's charity (Jn. 11:52) and burning concern for his sheep (Jn. 10). The profound love of Jesus (Jn. 2:25) transforms the missionary into a person of charity, a "universal brother," and a sign of God's all-

inclusive love in the world. Like Christ, the missionary must love the Church (Eph. 5:25) and be solicitous for her (II Cor. 11:28).

90.   Every Christian has a double vocation: *the universal call to holiness* which is closely linked to *the universal call to mission*. Thus, to be missionary means journeying toward holiness; the true missionary is, in a word, the saint. Renewing mission demands holy missioners; updated pastoral approaches and theology, while beneficial, must result in a new "ardor for holiness" among evangelizers. We should also recall the dynamism of the first Christians who preached Christ crucified (I Cor. 1:23).

91.   In a particular way young communities and young Churches are the hope and leaven of the Church – if they walk the path of holiness. Missionaries, too, should reflect on the duty of holiness required of them and become "contemplatives in action." In this way they can credibly proclaim Christ (I Jn. 1:1-3) – particularly in the Asian context. Finally, in imitation of Jesus, the missionary is a person of the Beatitudes (Mt. 5:1-12; 10) and proclaims "Good News" with the joy of one whose true hope is Christ.

CONCLUSION

92.   On the eve of the third millennium, the Church has a unique opportunity of bringing the Gospel to the world; a new missionary age is dawning. It calls for a response like that of the apostles (Acts 1:14) – one filled with generosity and holiness. It demands living more intensely the mystery of Christ and following the exemplary *path* of Mary, the Church's Mother and model.

Pope John Paul II concludes his message by entrusting the Church to Mary's mediation and extending his apostolic blessing in the name of the Trinity. The encyclical is dated December 7, 1990 on the twenty-fifth anniversary of the Conciliar Decree *Ad Gentes*.

Index